In Concert
Intermediate Violin Solos
or
Duets with Piano
for
Advent, Christmas, and the Holiday Season

by Angela Birkhead-Flight

Score

I0808770

WWW.MELBAY.COM

Preface

This collection of Advent and Christmas music includes some well-loved classics as well as pieces that will be new discoveries. While both beautiful and fun to play as duets, these pieces can also be performed as solo works using the Violin I part with the piano accompaniment. Each piece goes beyond a straightforward presentation of the main melody to bring a sense of joy and wonder to the music.

Joy to the World / The Ashplant
This exuberant hymn is paired with a snippet of the traditional fiddle tune "The Ashplant," an old-fashioned word for "walking stick." With harmonies winding their way both below and above the main melody, care should be taken to allow the melody to be heard clearly.

O Come, O Come Emmanuel
The light jazz syncopation paired with large dynamic contrasts and soaring improvisatory passages creates a more modern sound for this ancient melody while still conveying a sense of anticipation.

Pat-a-Pan
The crisp quarter note rhythm invoking the drum mentioned in the original lyrics is contrasted with an original lyrical middle section with a soaring melody. This piece has call and answer phrases between the piano and strings that make it a fun collaboration.

Gabriel's Message / Cold Frosty Morning
The 3/4 meter of this mystical, medieval hymn is paired with the toe-tapping 4/4 fiddle tune, invoking the sense of the joy underlying the visit from the angel.

Angels We Have Heard on High
After an introductory pensive verse, this arrangement breaks into a joyful, syncopated collaboration between piano and strings. Followed by a soaring countermelody, there is much opportunity for expression.

Silent Night
The gentle piano part and descending countermelody in the Violin 1 part evoke the gentle falling of snow.

Snowfall
Inspired by Erik Satie's famous work, this piece offers a challenge to the violinist, requiring very controlled bow distribution.

St. Basil's Hymn
Beginning "sul D, sul tasto," this arrangement uses light bow pressure to add to the mysterious nature of this ancient Greek melody. This is contrasted with a section of original music incorporating a richer tone.

O Holy Night
A straight-forward presentation of the hymn is followed by an improvisatory restatement. The dramatic nature of this piece is aided by large dynamic contrasts and a rising scale pattern beneath the main melody.

What Child Is This?
With its sudden shifts in both tempo and mood, this arrangement of "What Child Is This?" reflects the original text of this carol rather than that found in modern hymnals. Beginning as a lullaby, the second verse reflects the pain that is to come ("Nails, spears, shall pierce him through"). A more fiddle-like ending suggests the joy of the epiphany, creating an opportunity to tell a dramatic story with the music.

Angela Birkhead-Flight

About the Author

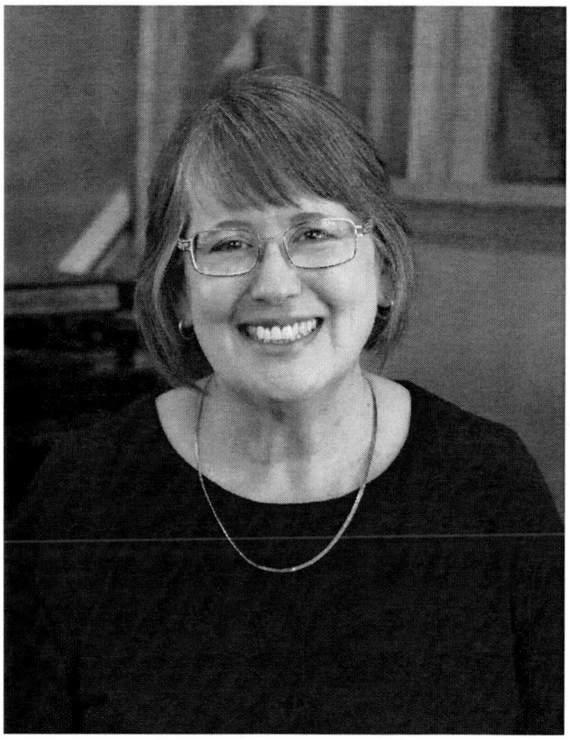

American composer and musician Angela Birkhead-Flight began working as a church musician in high school and continued while attending Saint Mary-of-the-Woods College in Indiana. She has held positions directing music at parishes in Indiana, California, and Ohio. Birkhead-Flight earned advanced degrees in experimental and research psychology at California State University Long Beach and the University of Cincinnati. After several years of teaching college, she returned to church music, and is currently the director of music at Cheviot United Methodist Church. She is a composer of music for organ, piano, violin, various other instruments, and is an award-winning choral composer.

Contents

Joy to the World / The Ashplant

"Antioch" by Lowell Mason / Trad. Fiddle Tune
Arr. Angela Birkhead-Flight

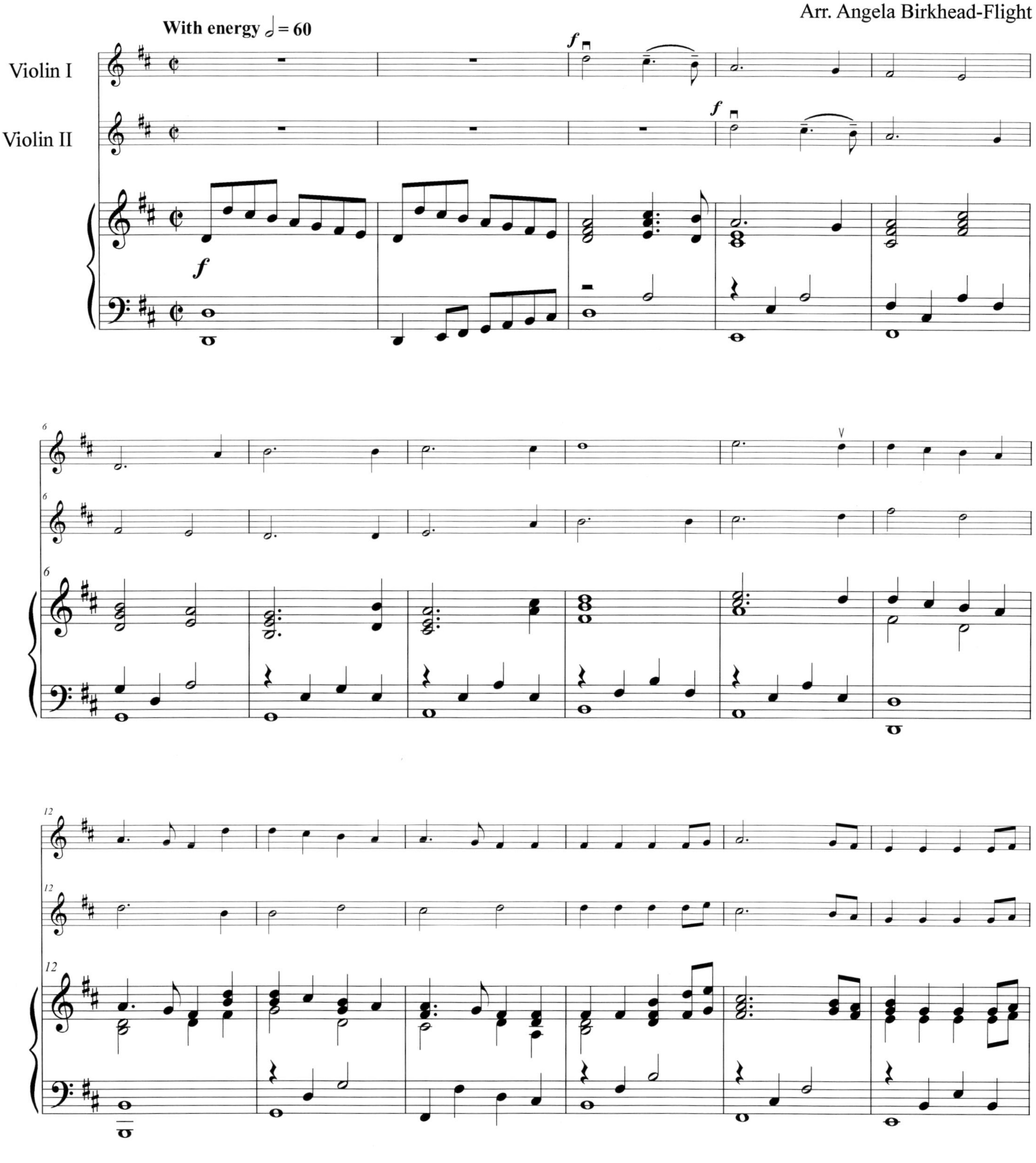

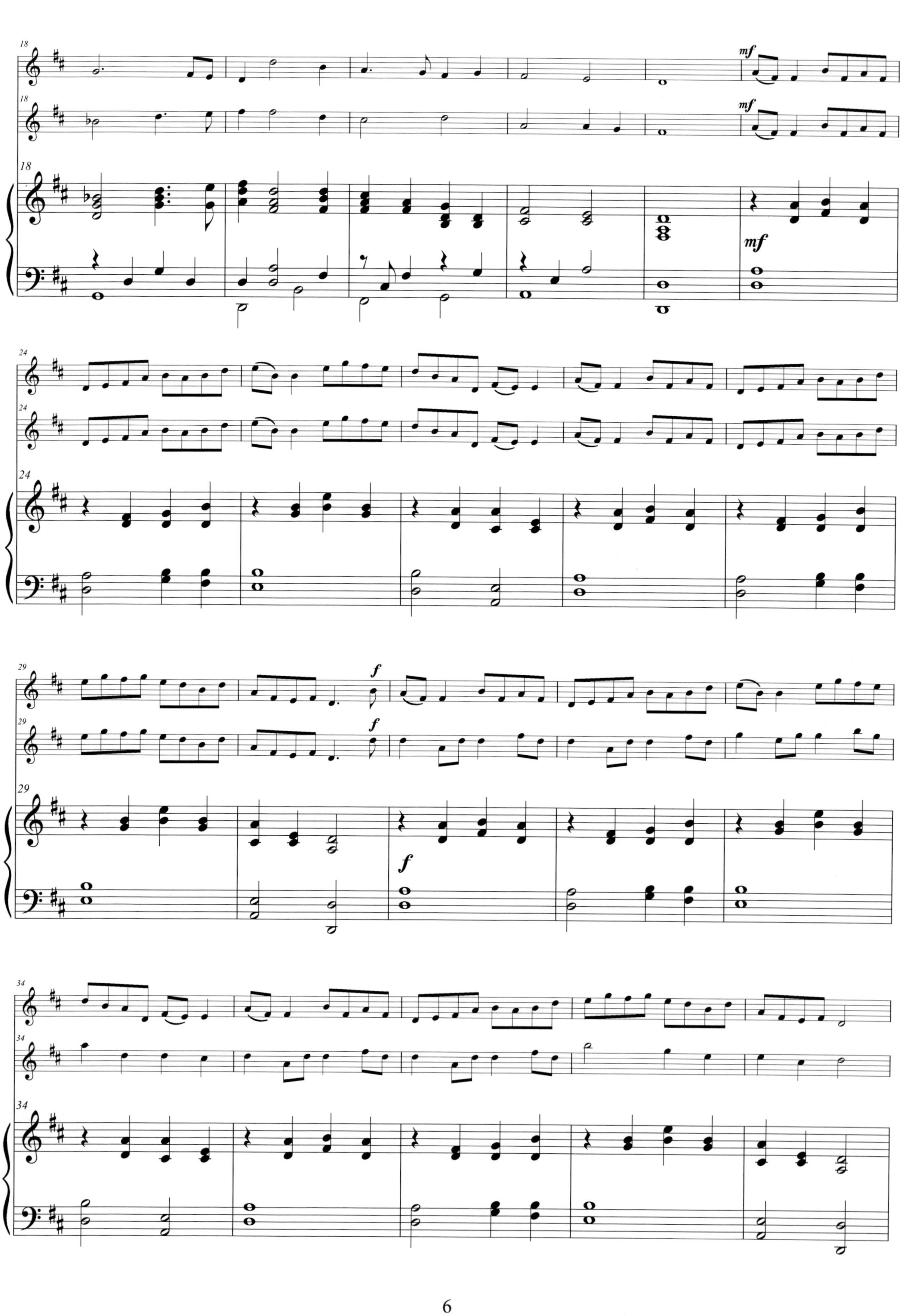
mf
f

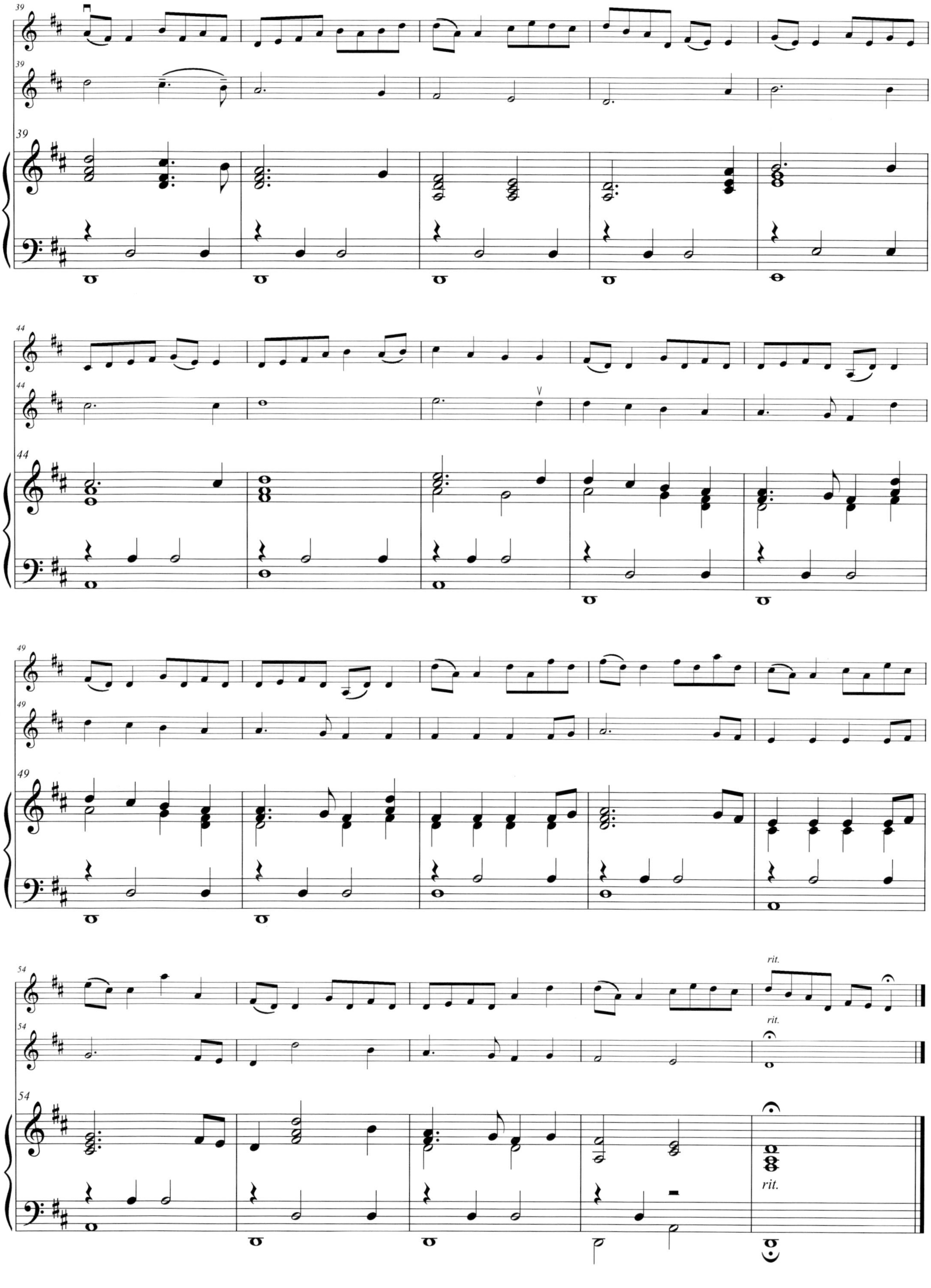
rit.
rit.
rit.

O Come, O Come Emmanuel

French, 15th century
Arr. Angela Birkhead-Flight

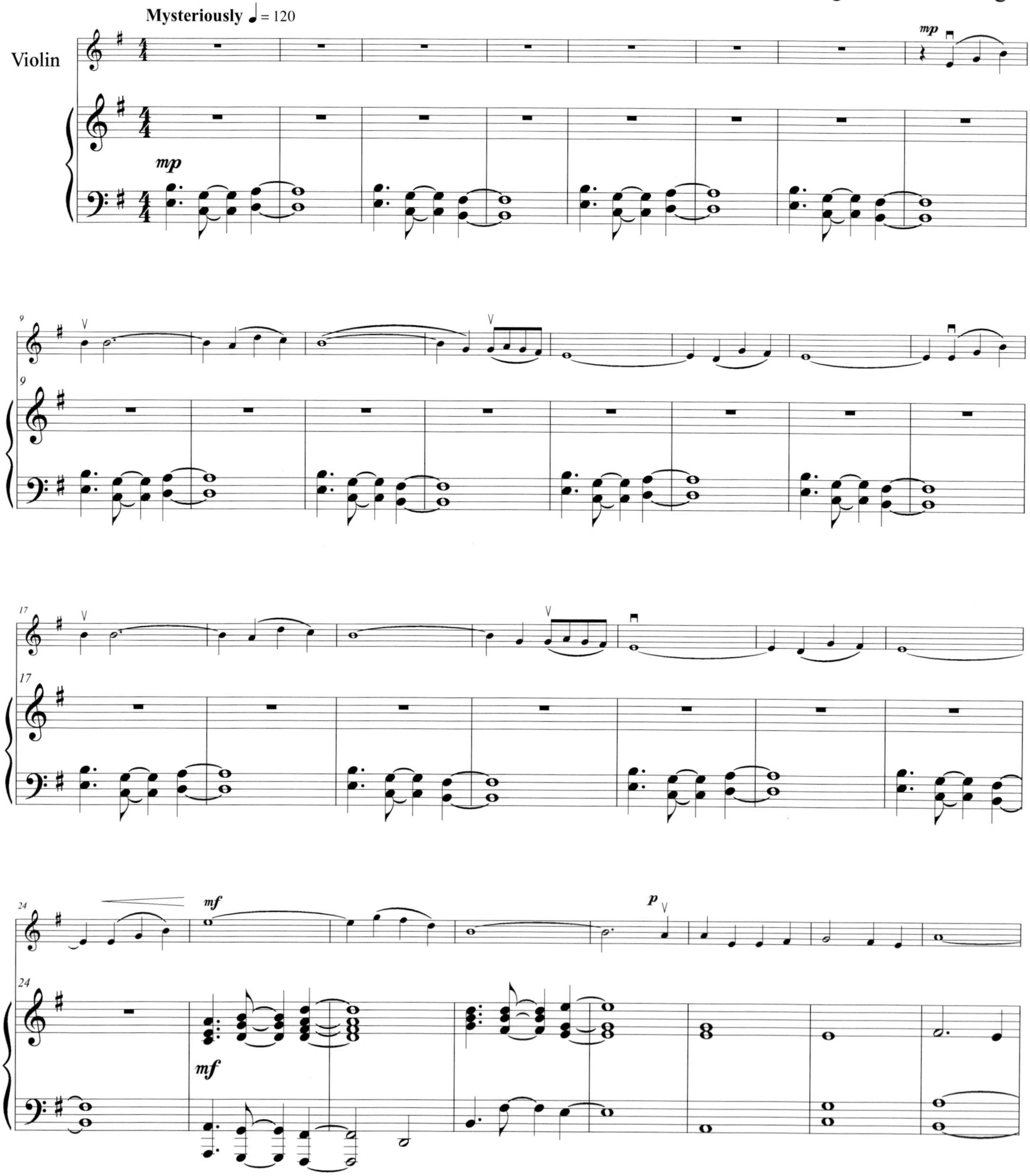

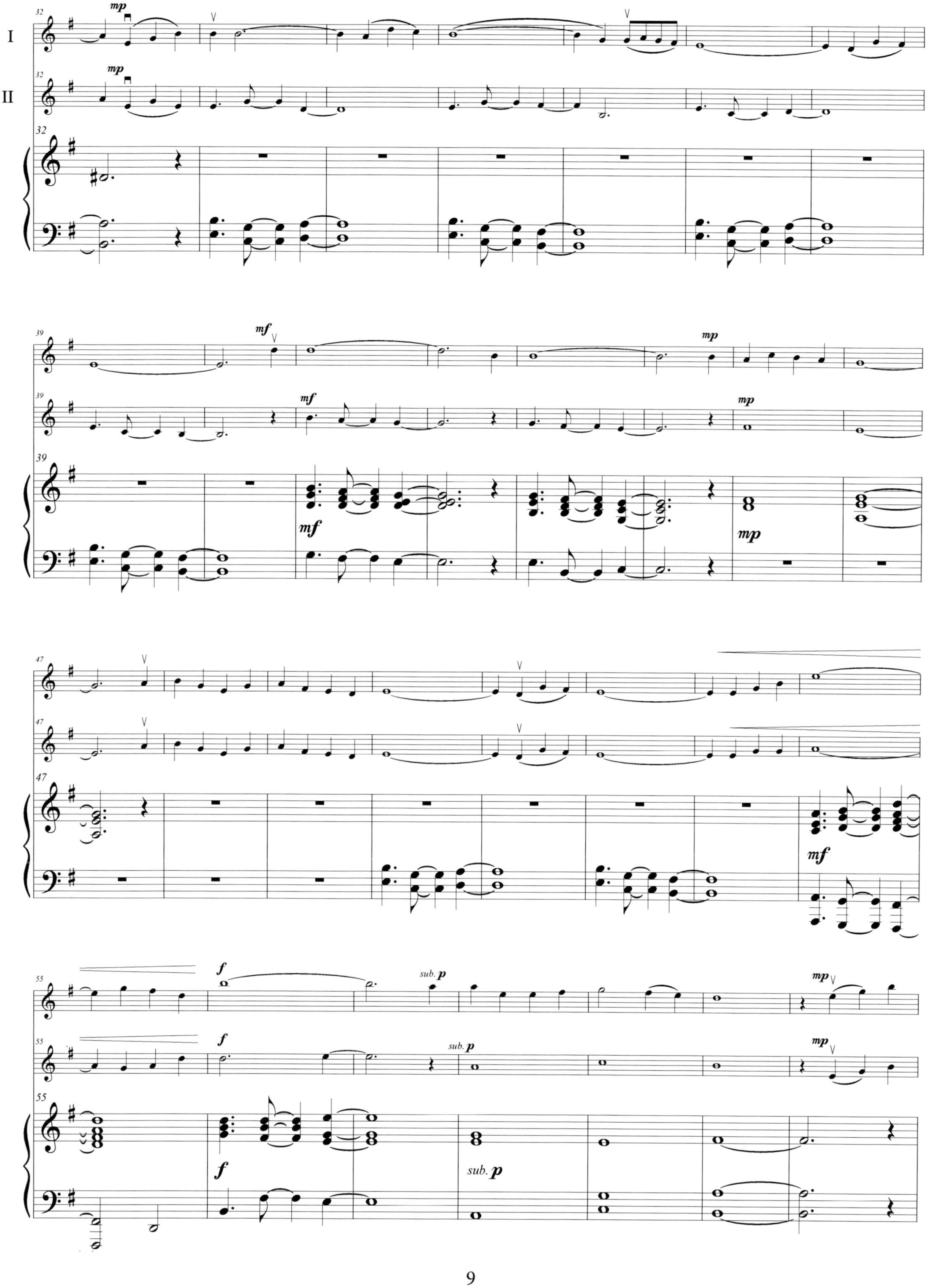
I
II
mp
mf
f
sub. p

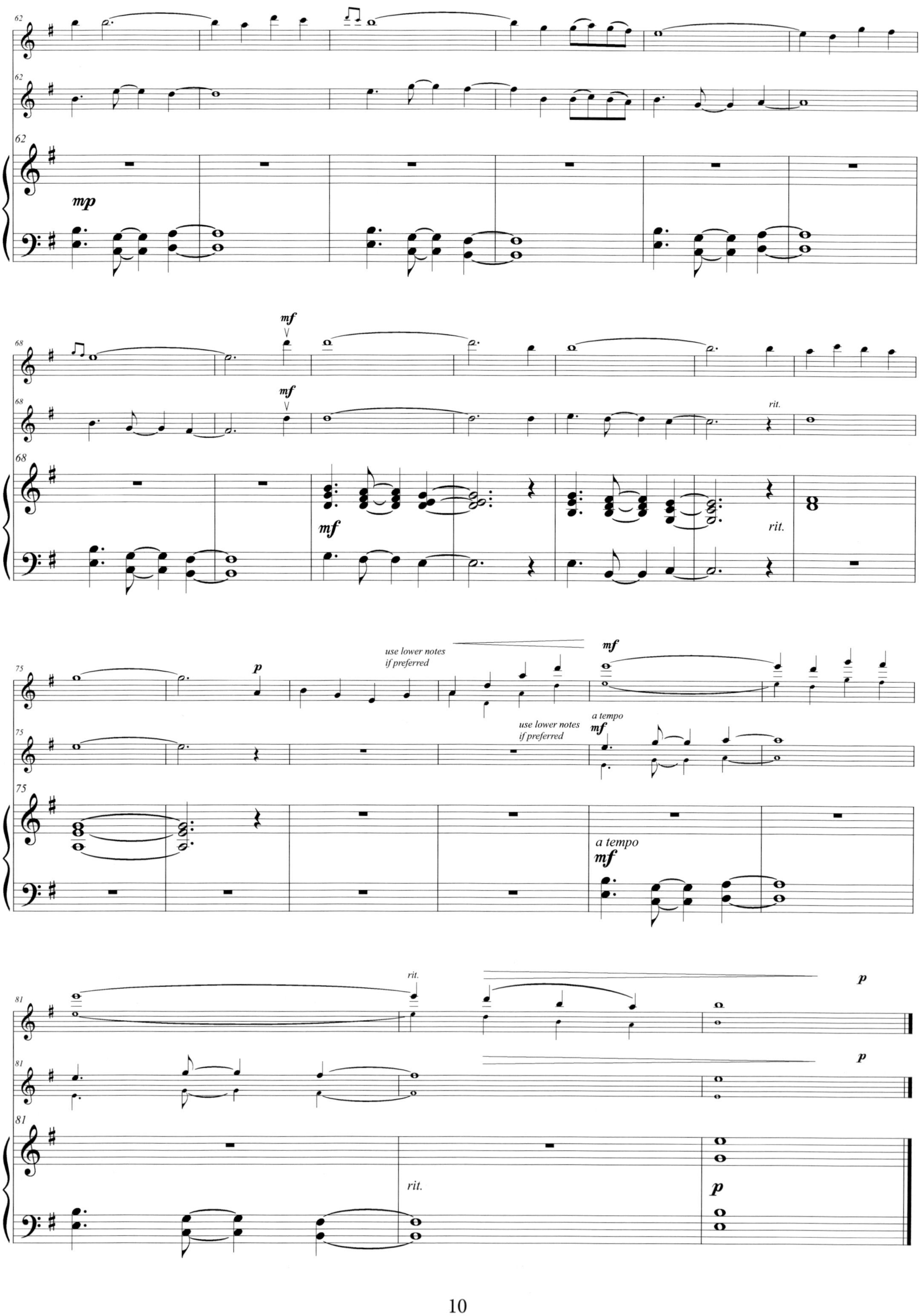
mp
mf
rit.
use lower notes
if preferred
a tempo
p

Pat-a-Pan

Bernard de La Monnoye (1641–1728)
Arr. Angela Birkhead-Flight

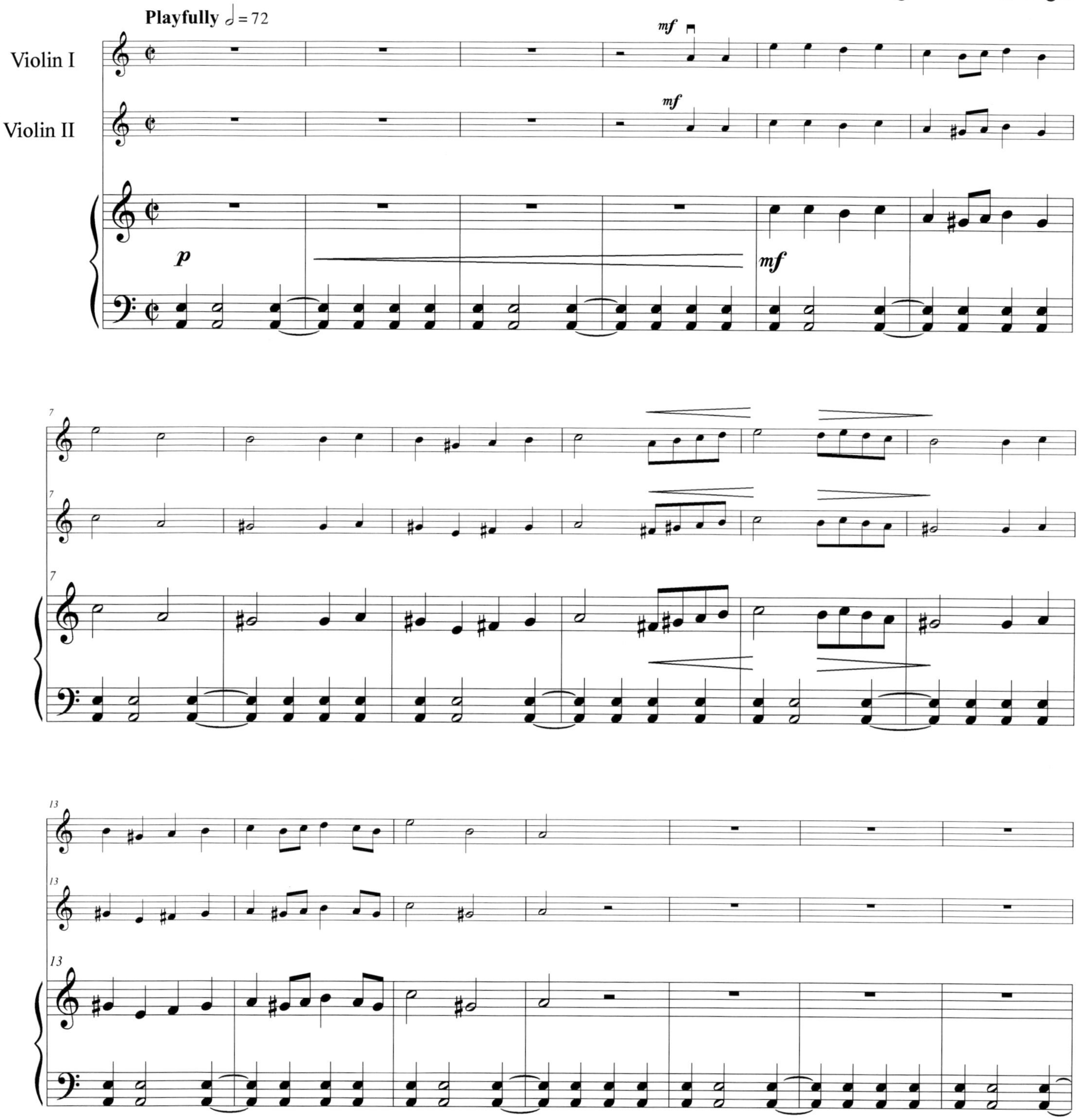

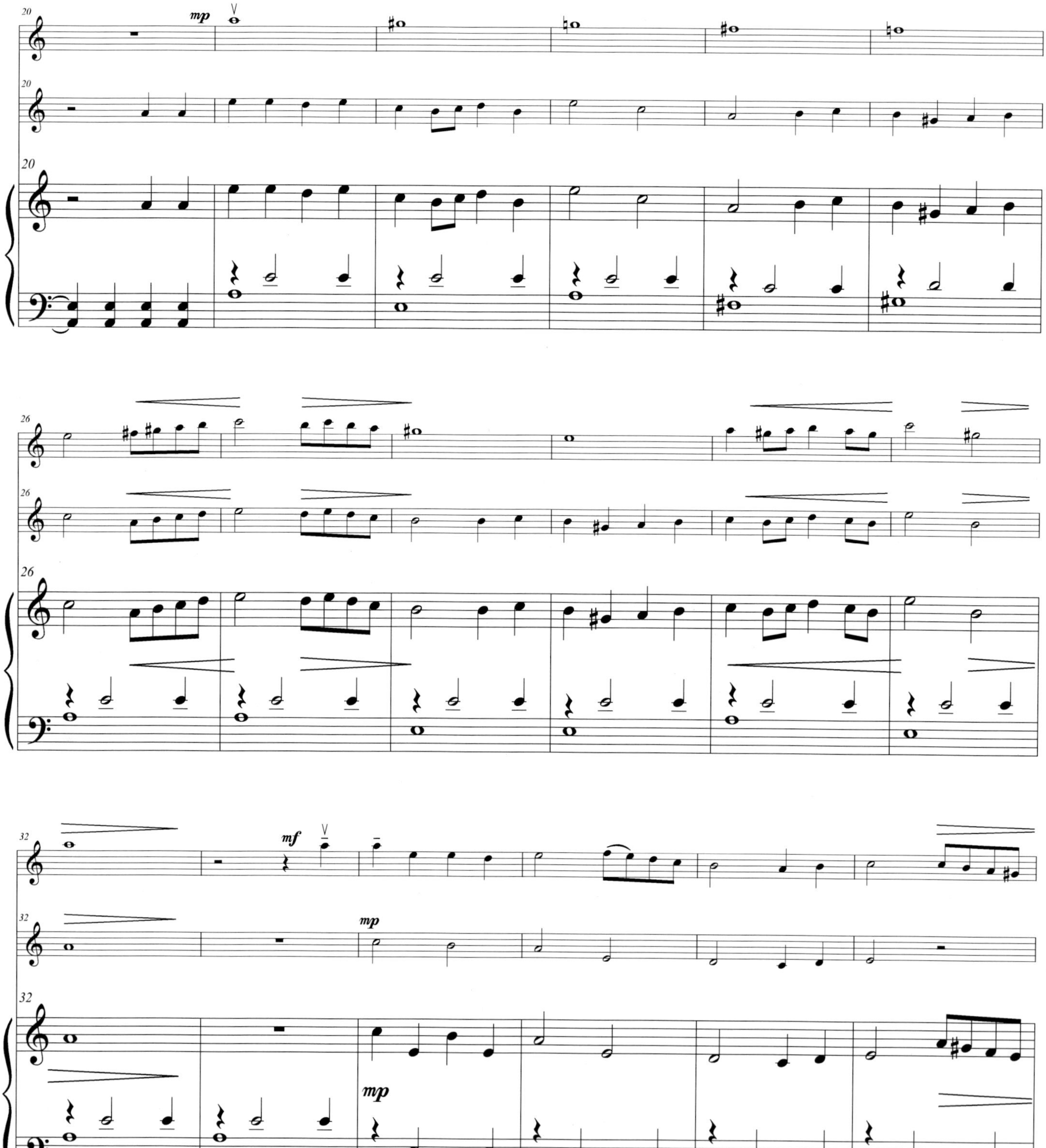
20
mp
26
32
mf
mp

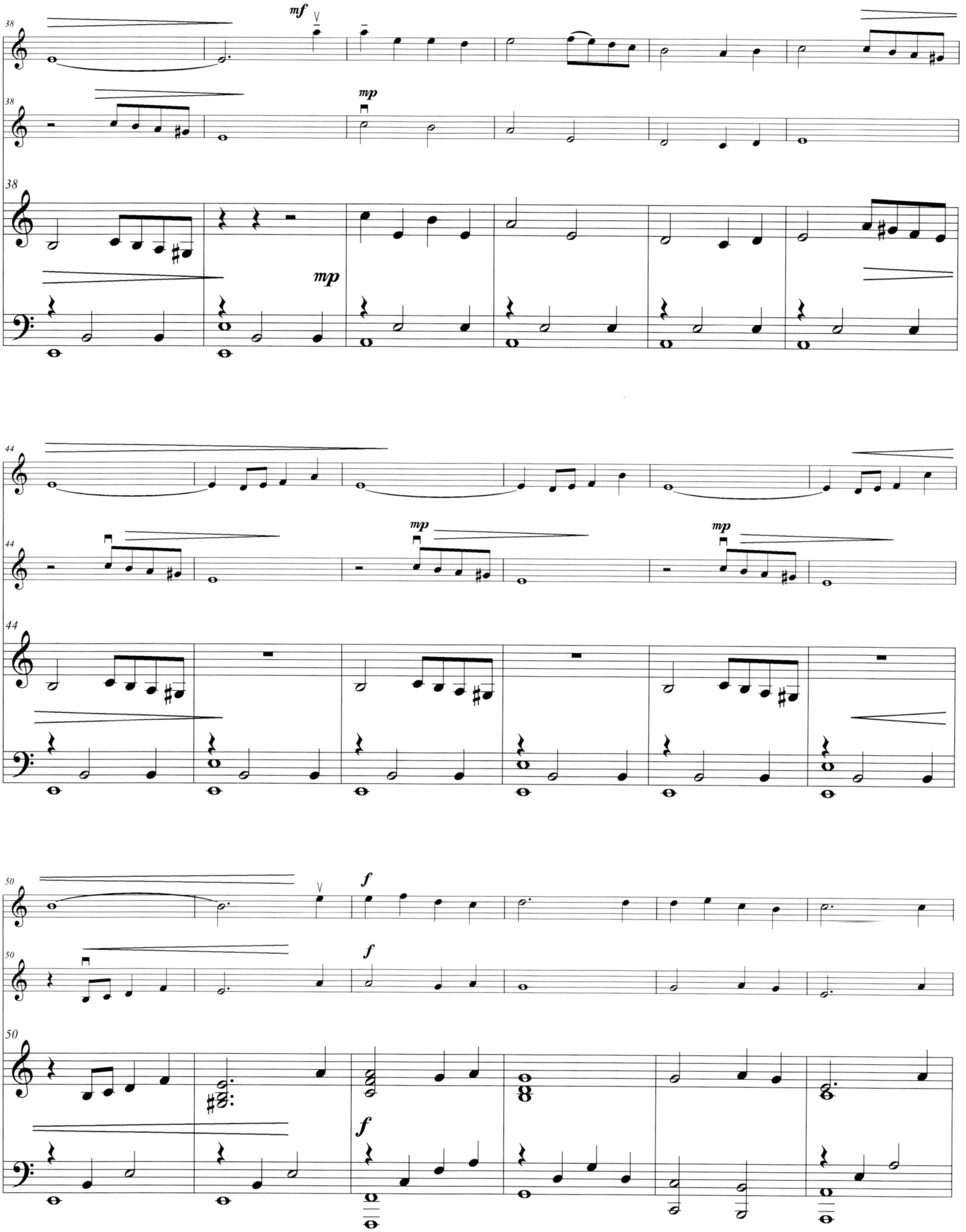
38
mf
mp
44
mp
mp
50
f
f
f

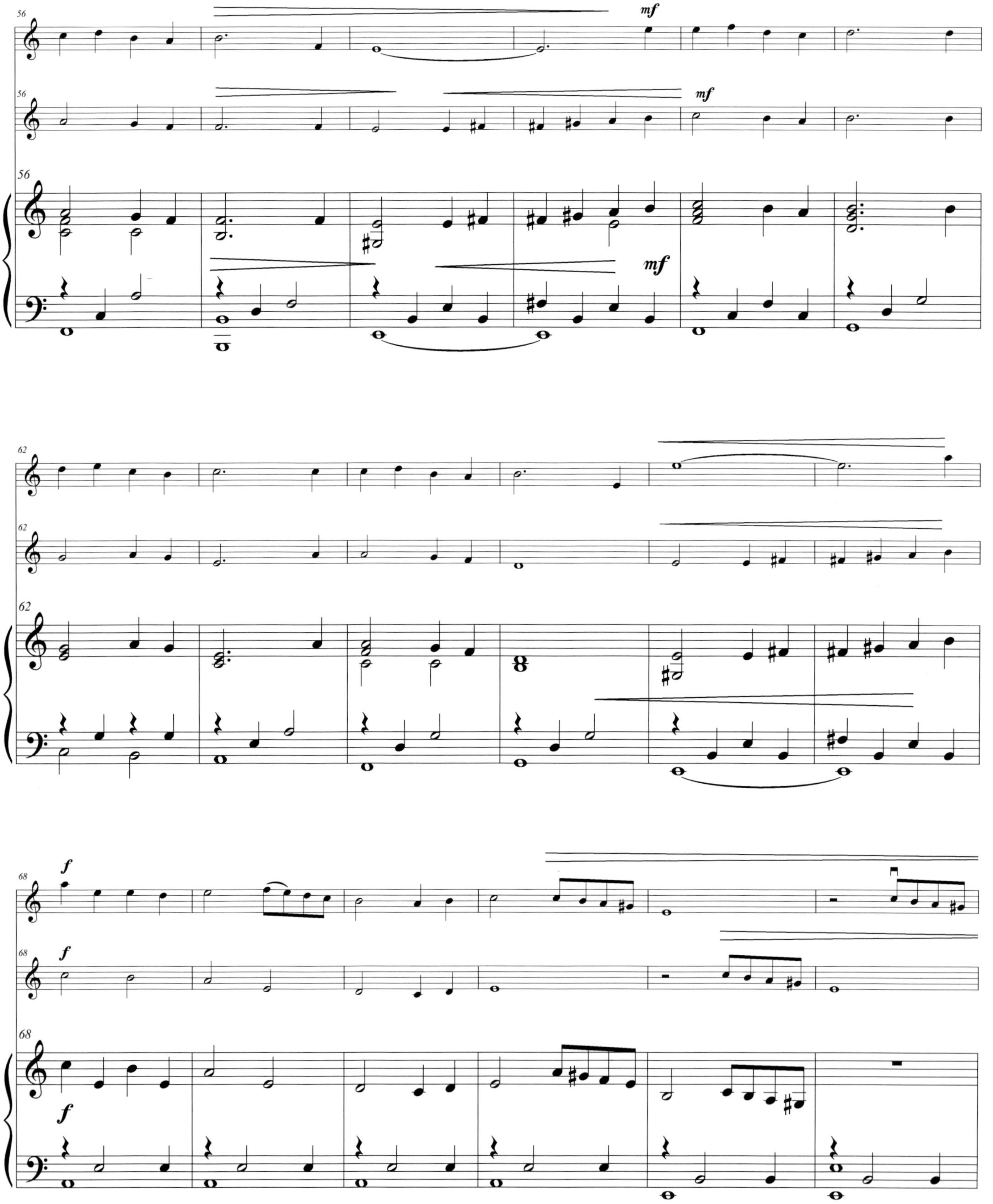
56
mf
mf
mf
62
68
f
f
f

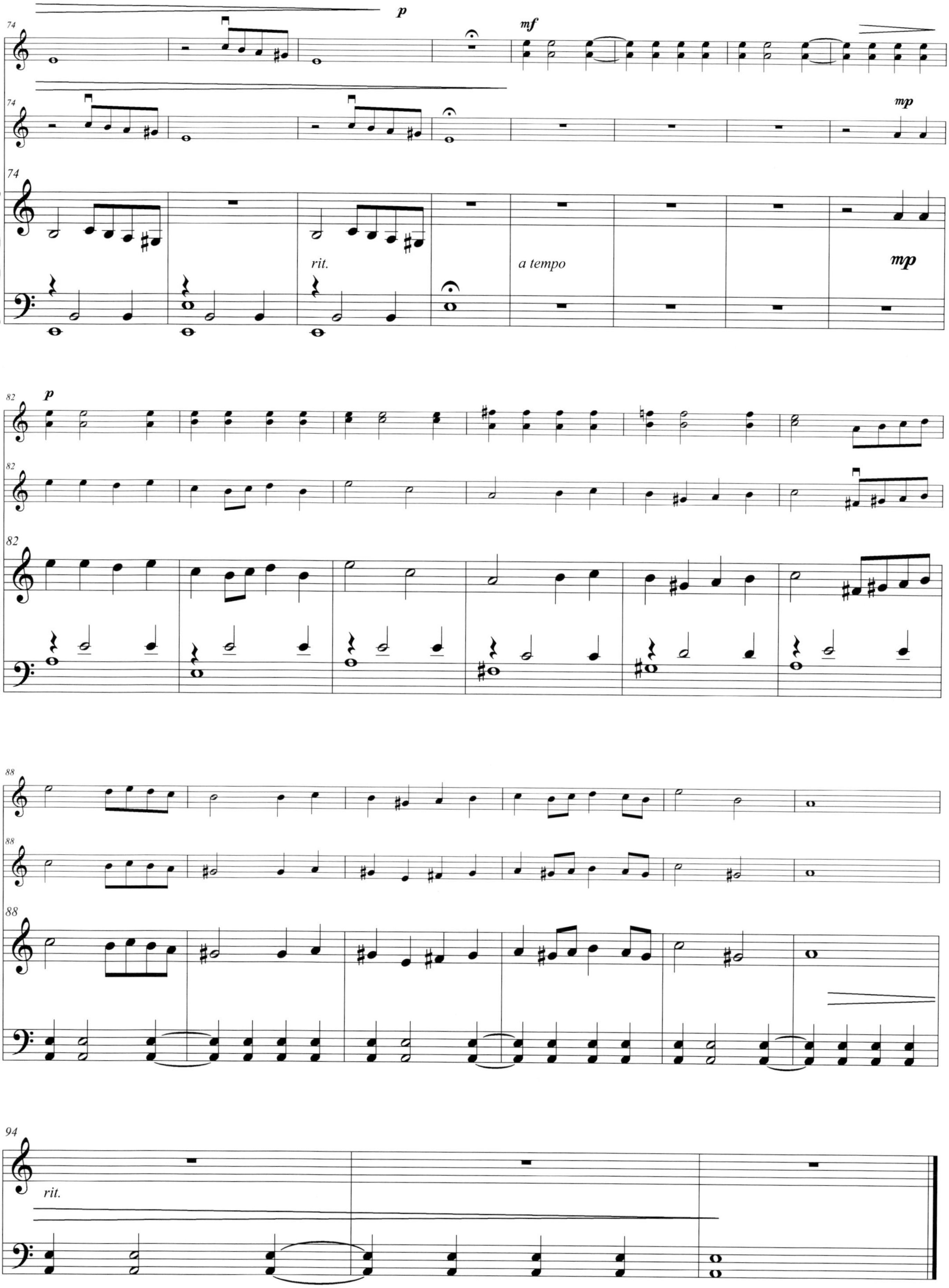
74
p
mf
mp
rit.
a tempo
mp
82
p
88
94
rit.

Gabriel's Message / Cold Frosty Morning

Basque Folk Carol / American Fiddle Tune
Arr. Angela Birkhead-Flight

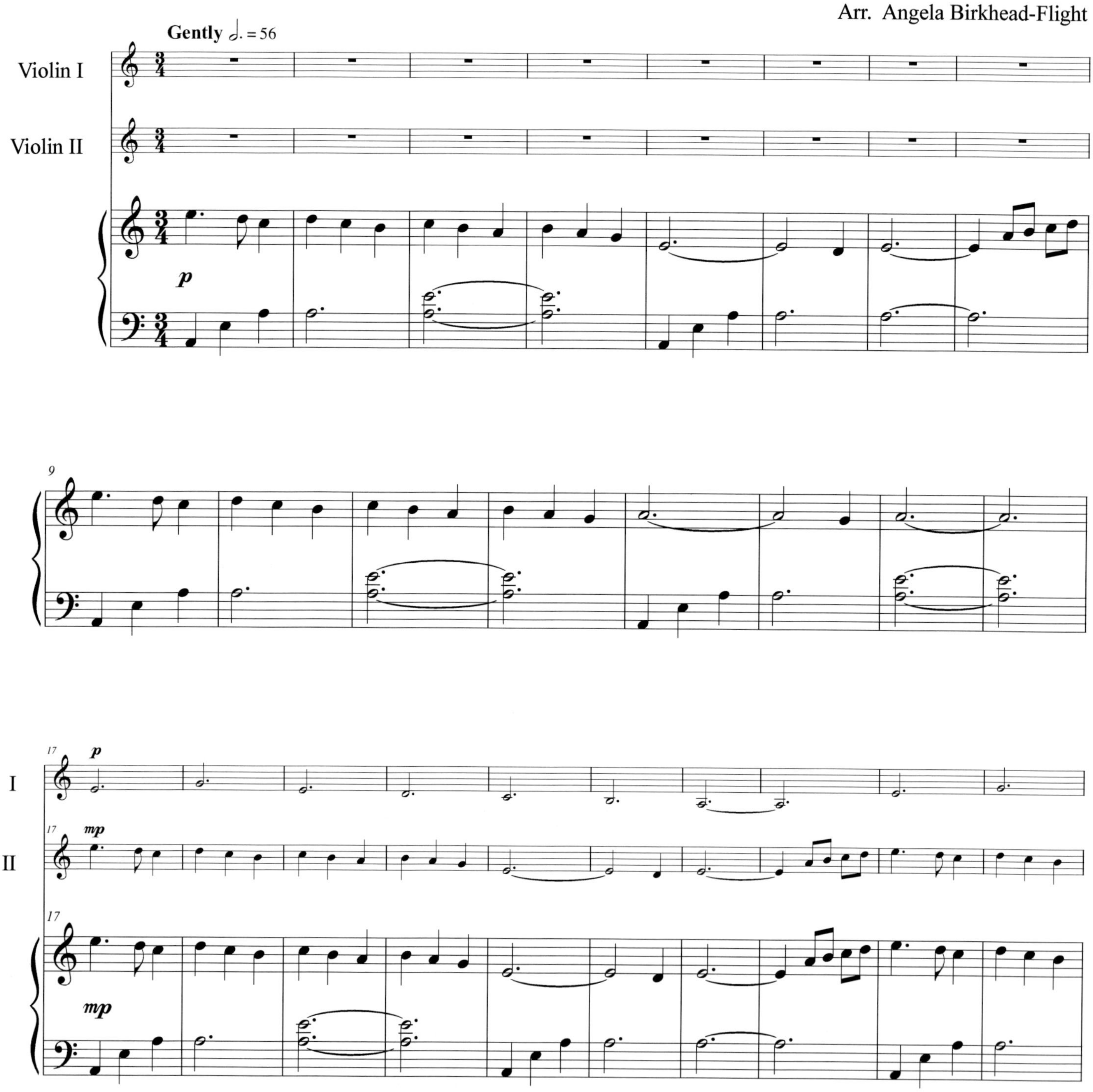

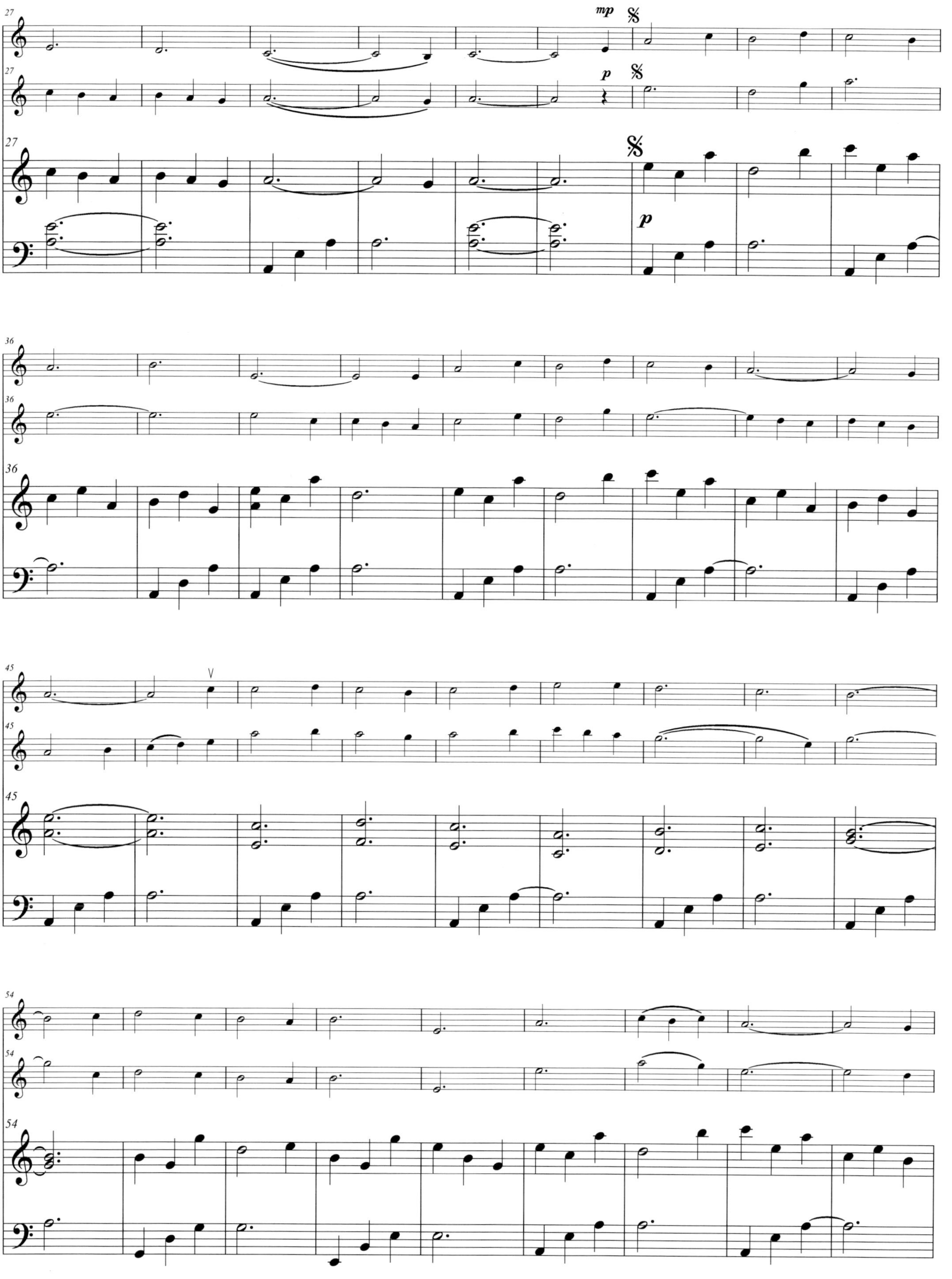
mp
p
p

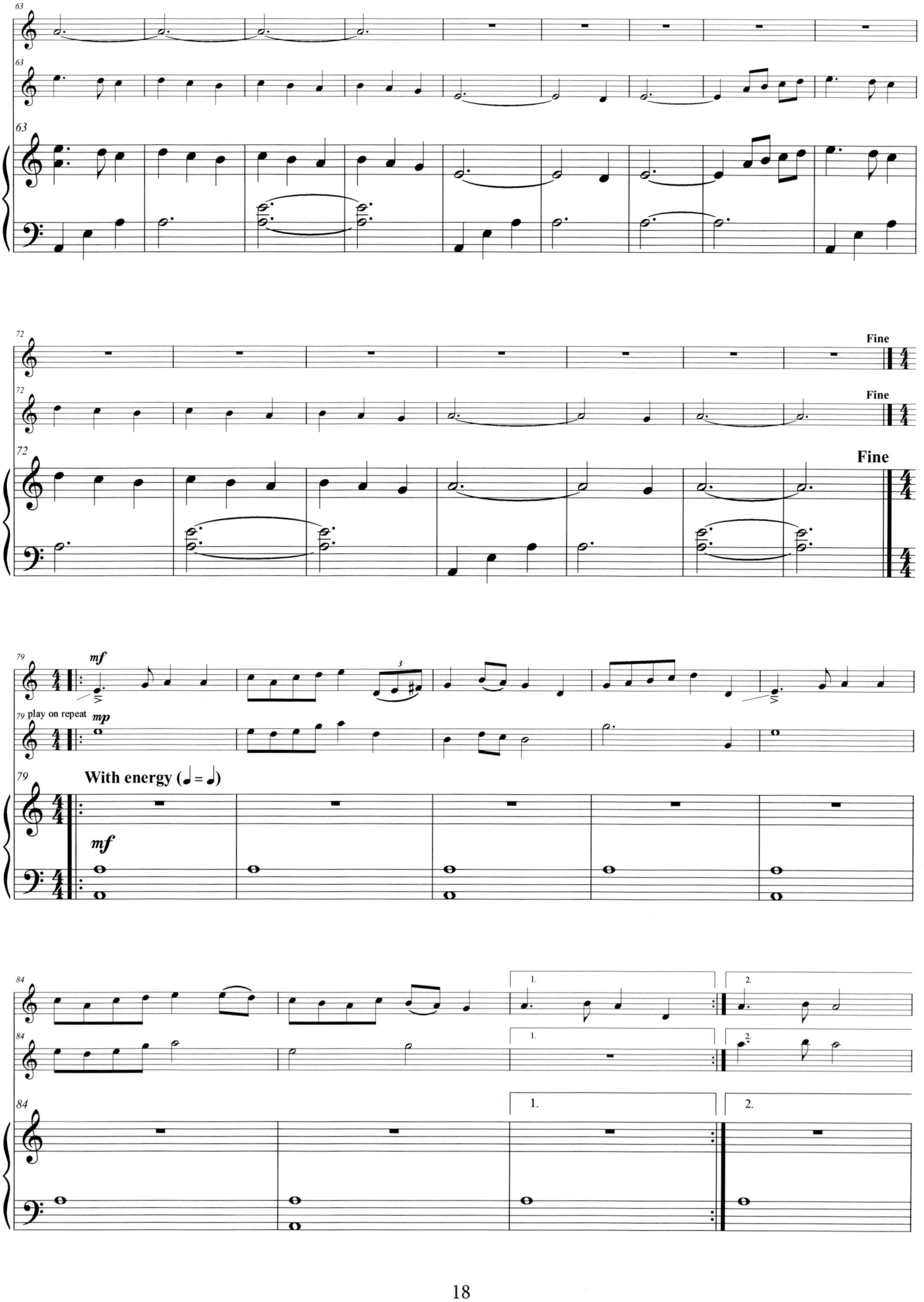
Fine
Fine
Fine
mf
play on repeat
mp
With energy (♩ = ♩)
mf
1.
2.
1.
2.
1.
2.

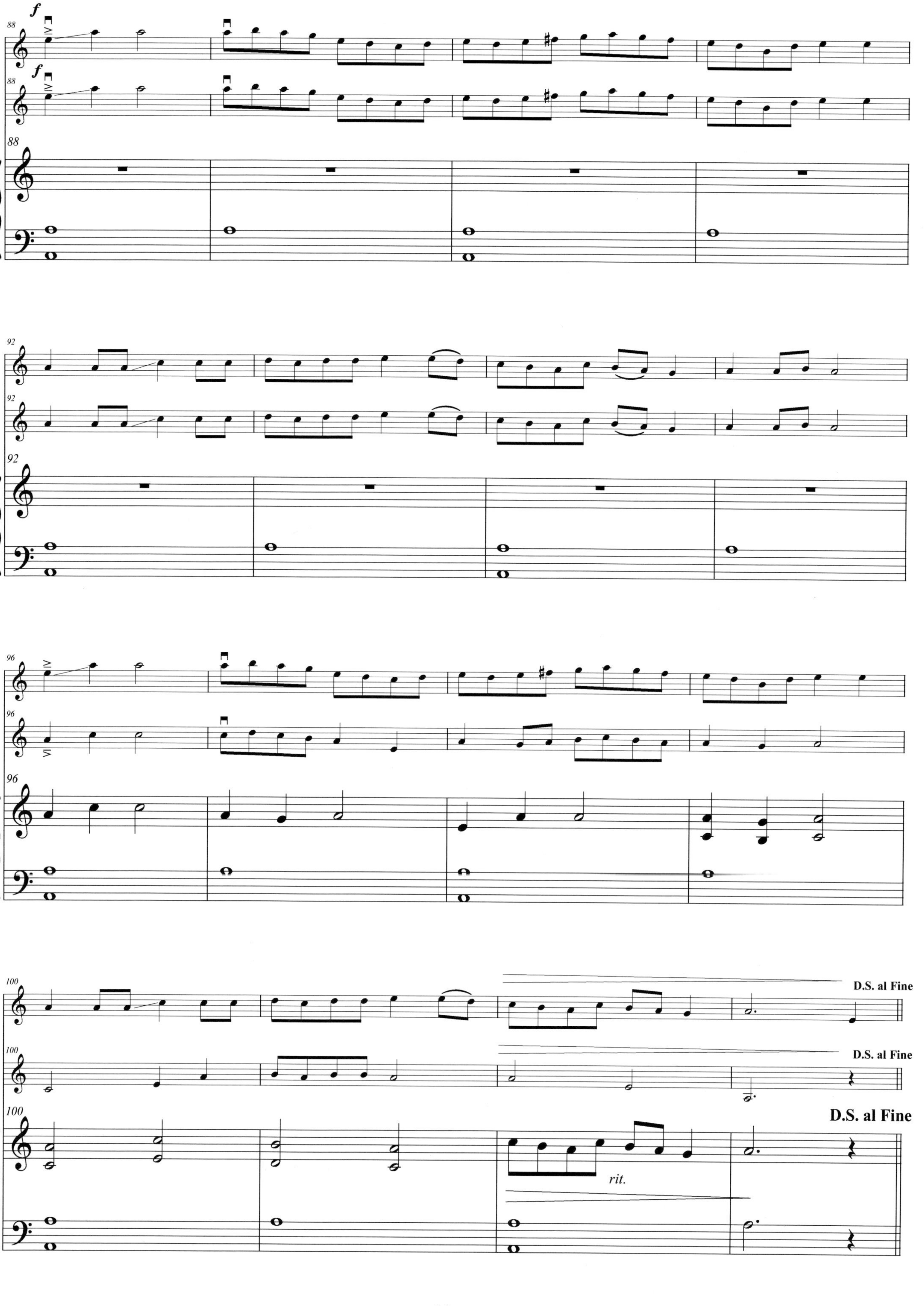
f
f
rit.
D.S. al Fine
D.S. al Fine
D.S. al Fine

Angels We Have Heard on High

Traditional French Carol
Arr. Angela Birkhead-Flight

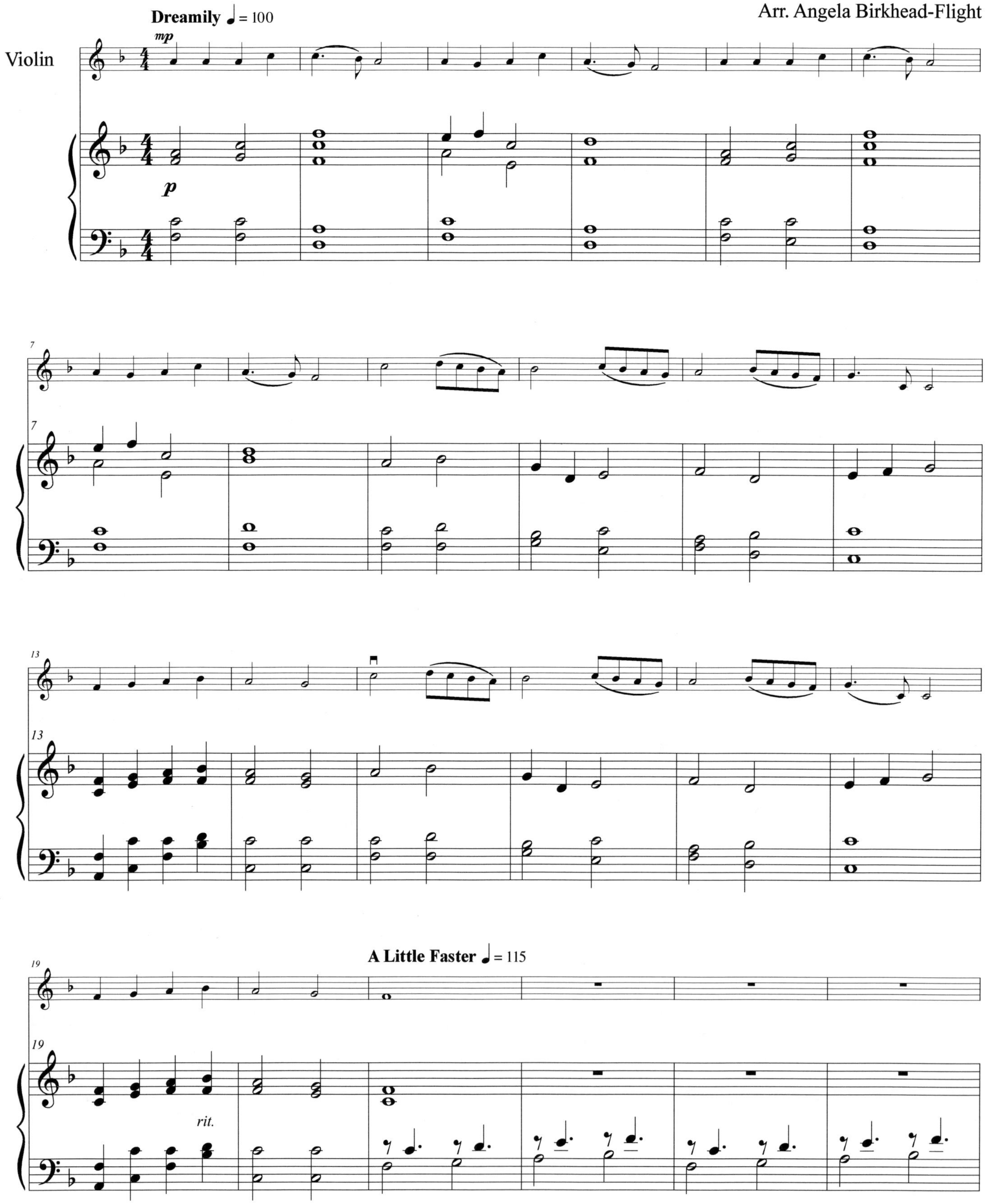

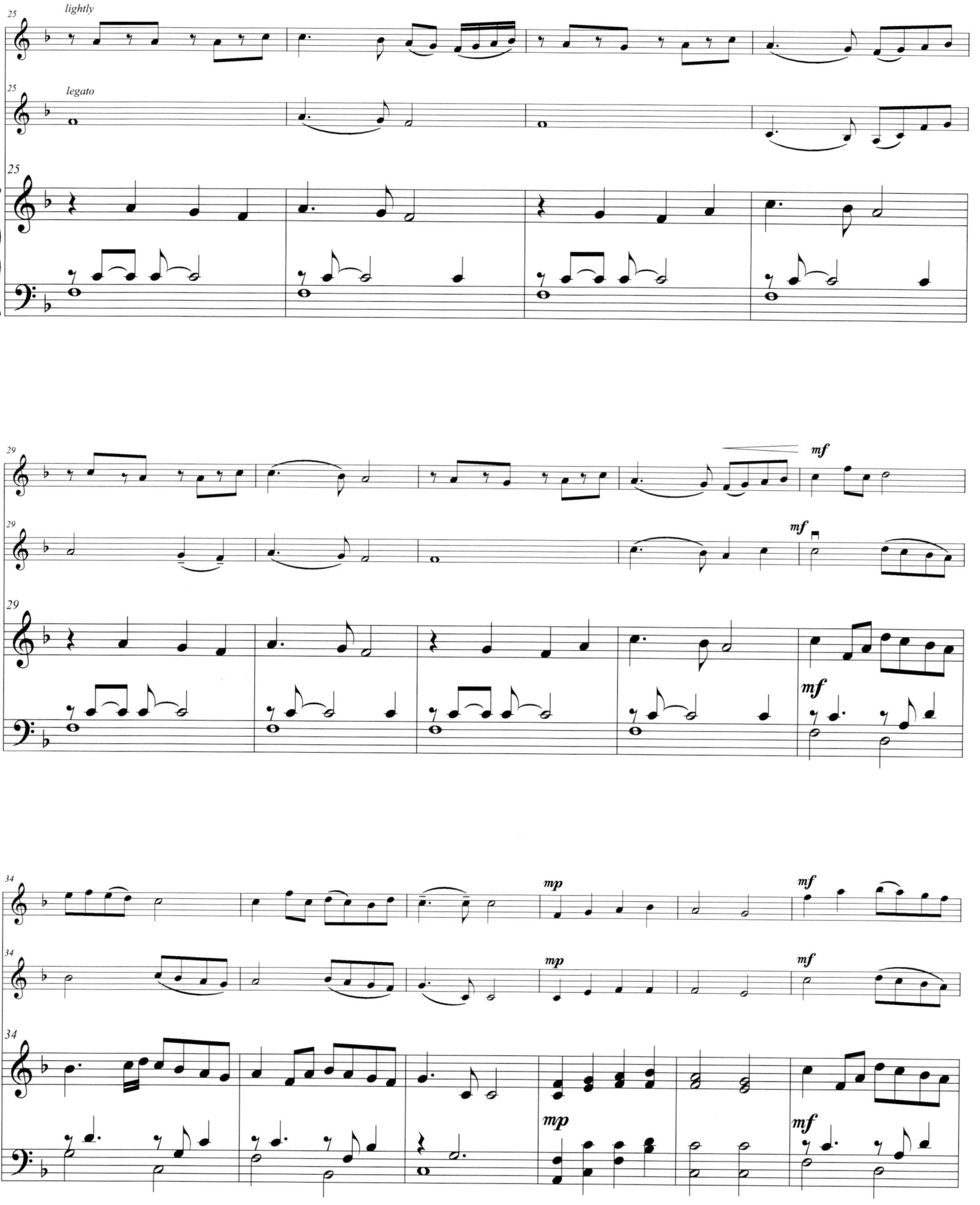
lightly
I
legato
II
mf
mp

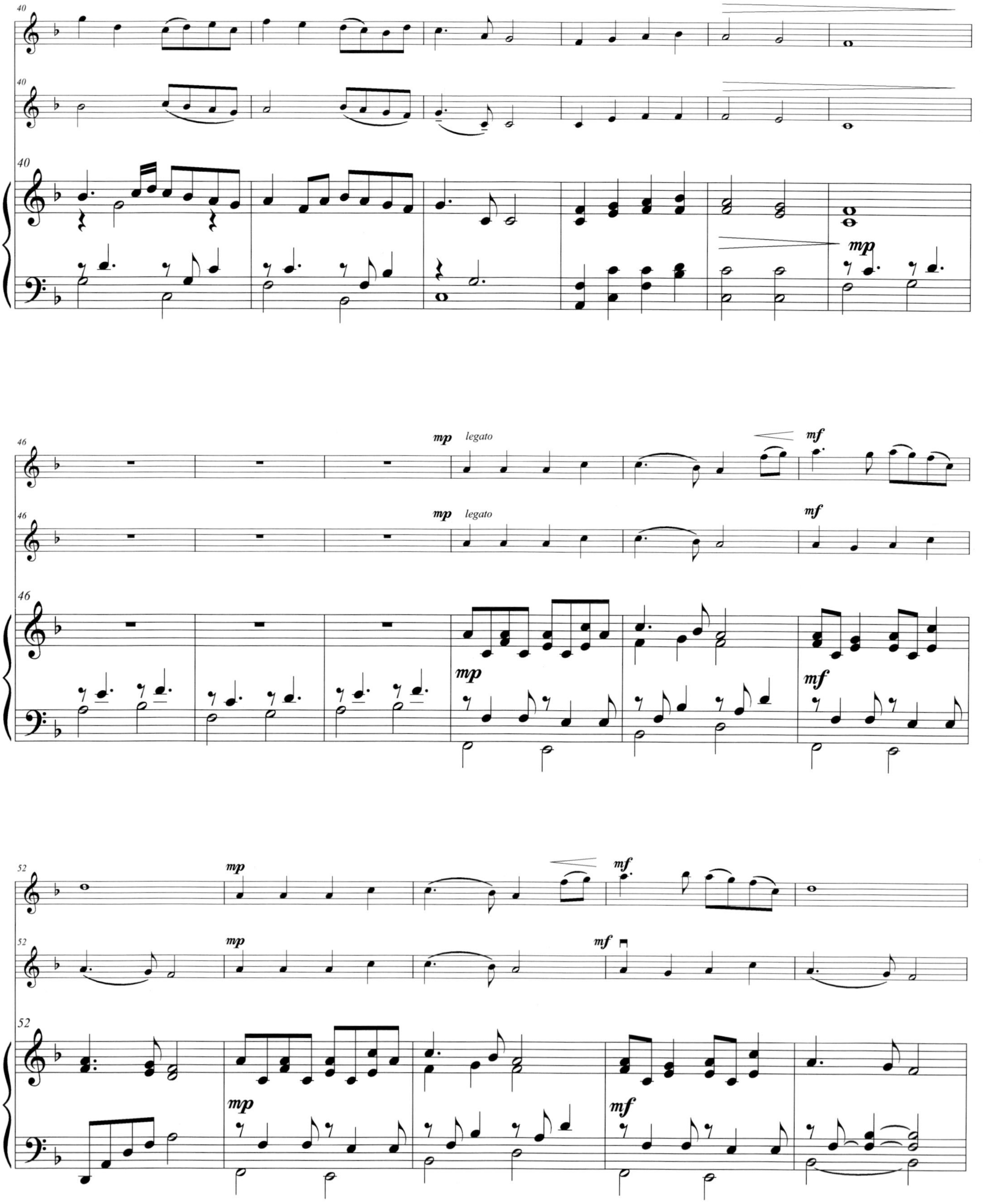
mp
legato
mf

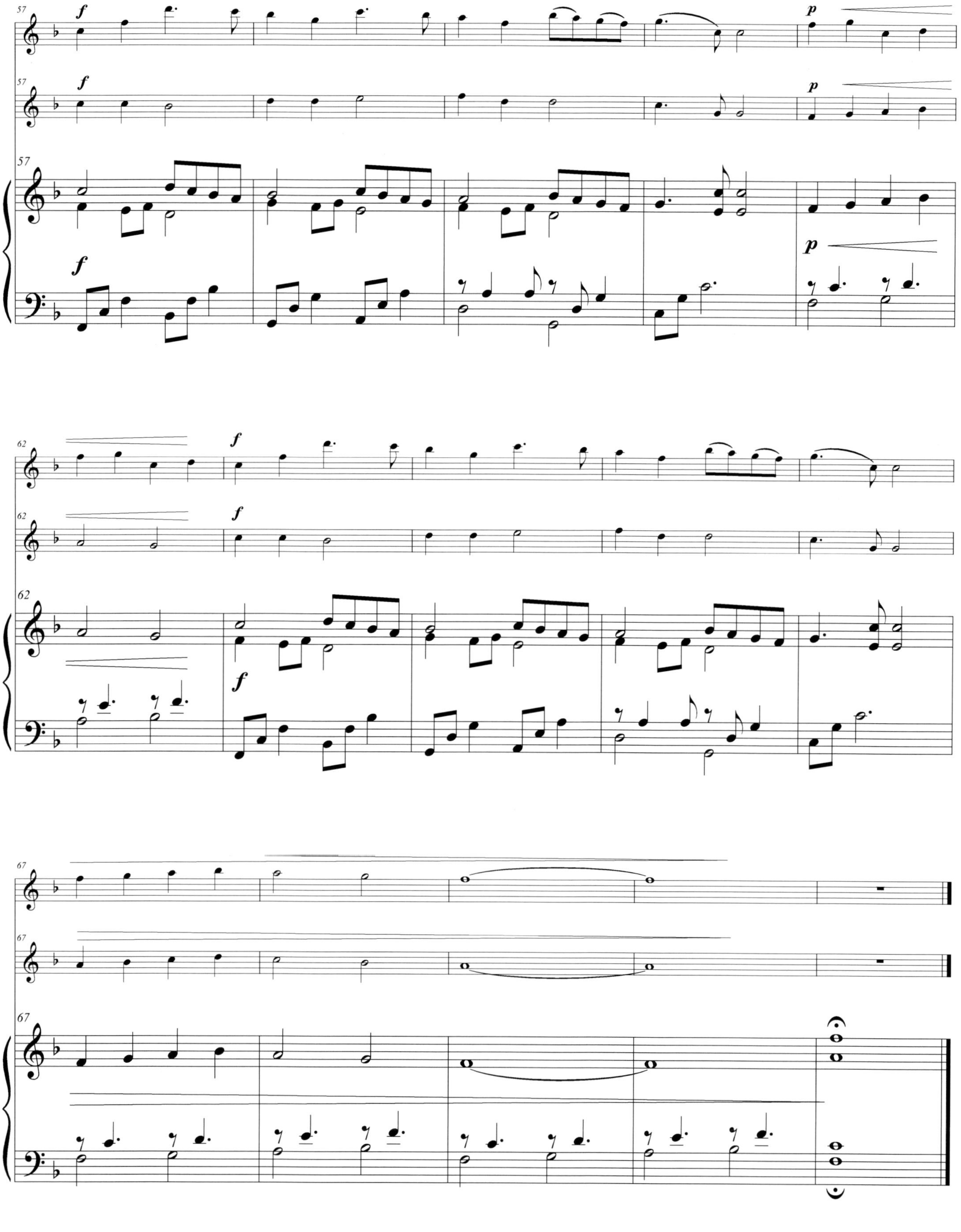

Silent Night

Franz Gruber
Arr. Angela Birkhead-Flight

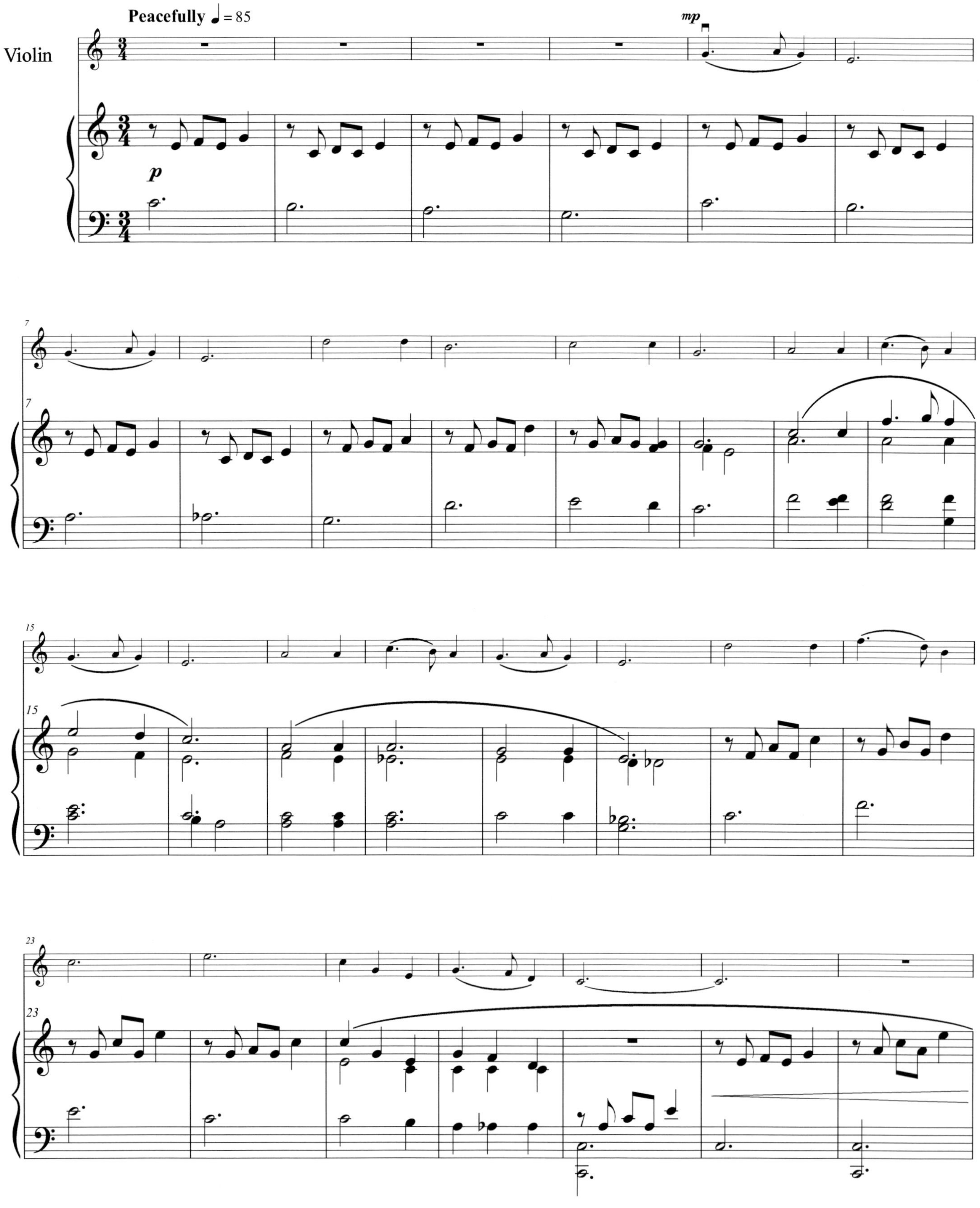

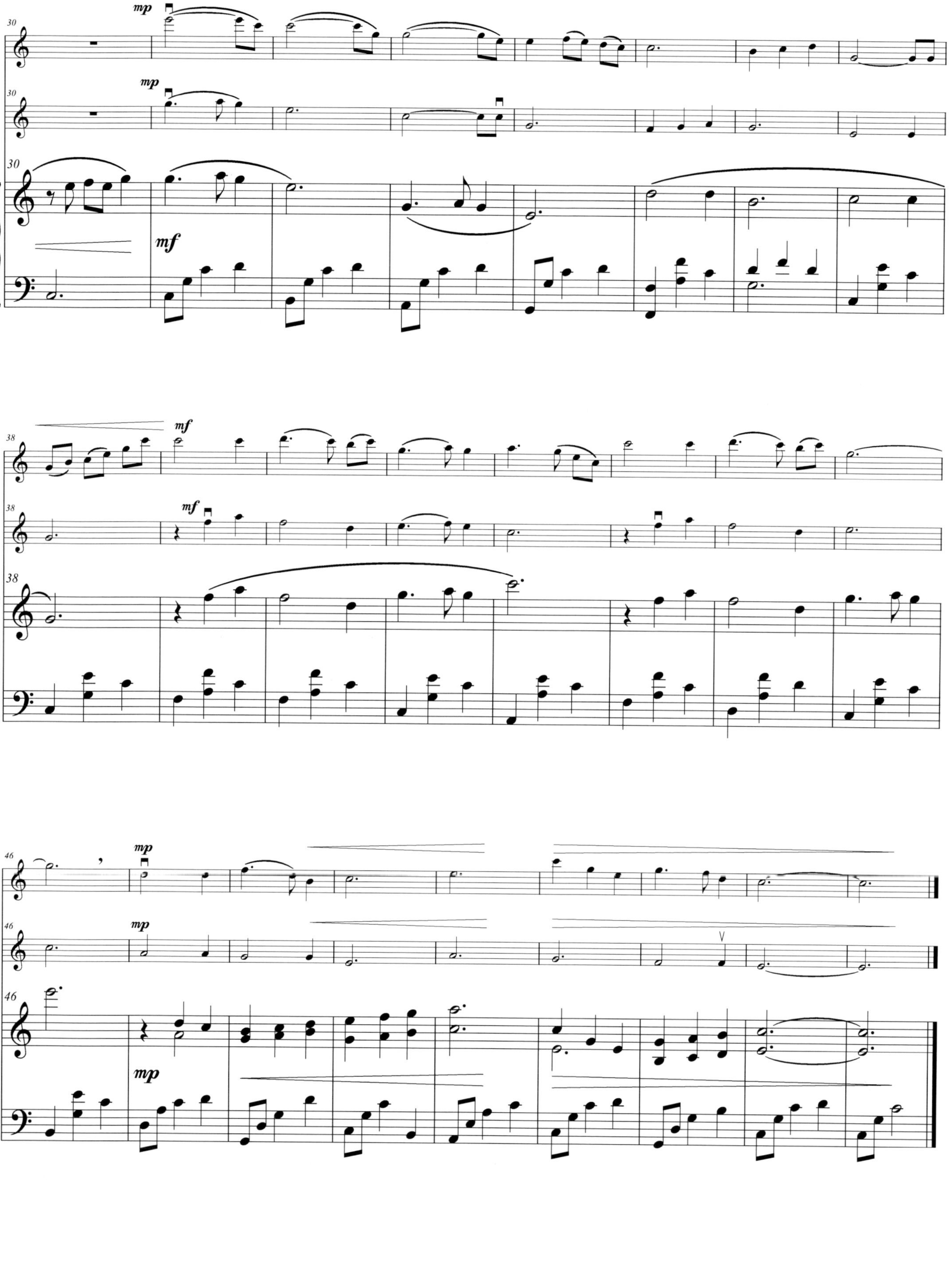
I
II
30
mp
mf
38
46

Snowfall

Inspired by Gymnopédie No. 1
by Erik Satie
Angela Birkhead-Flight

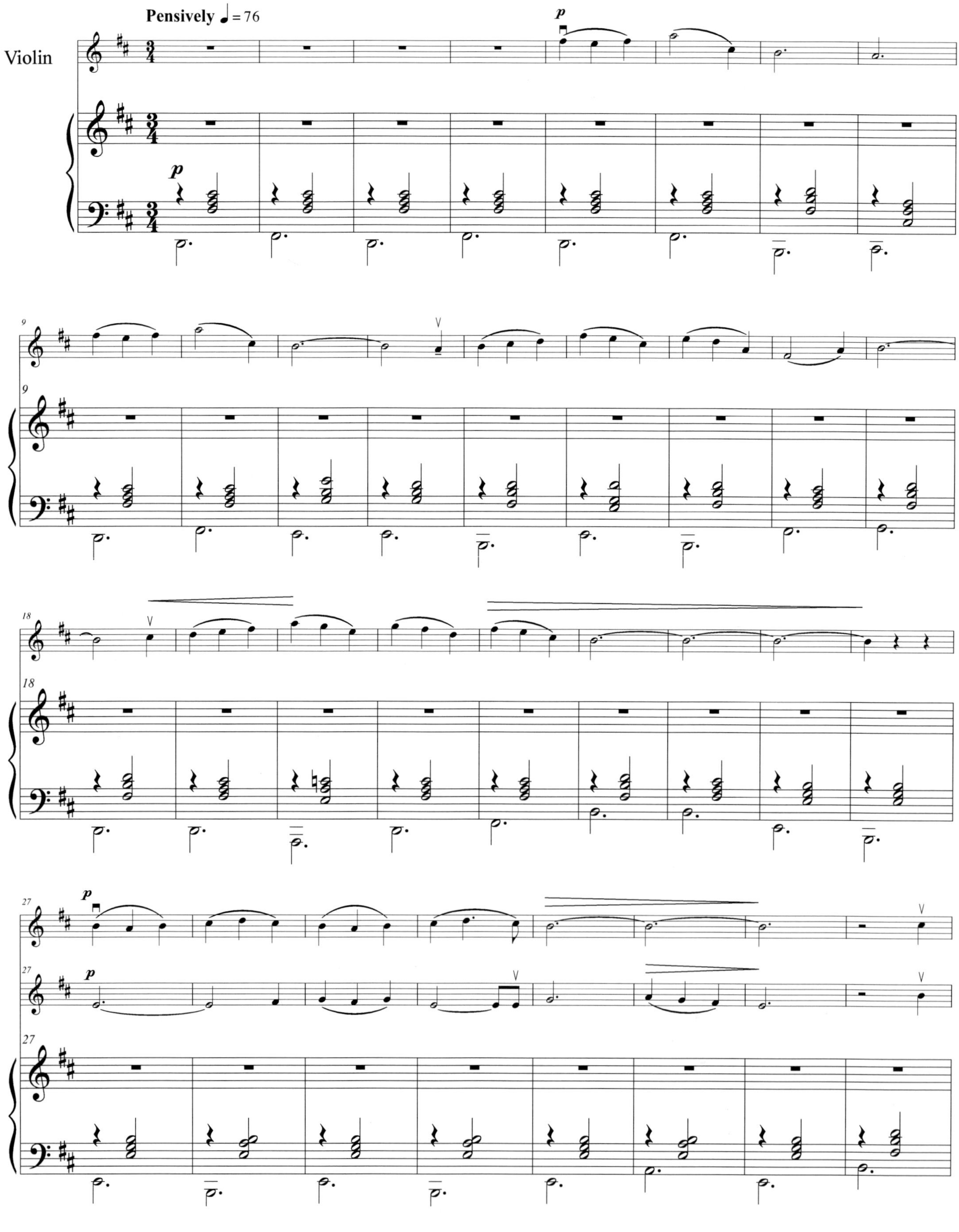

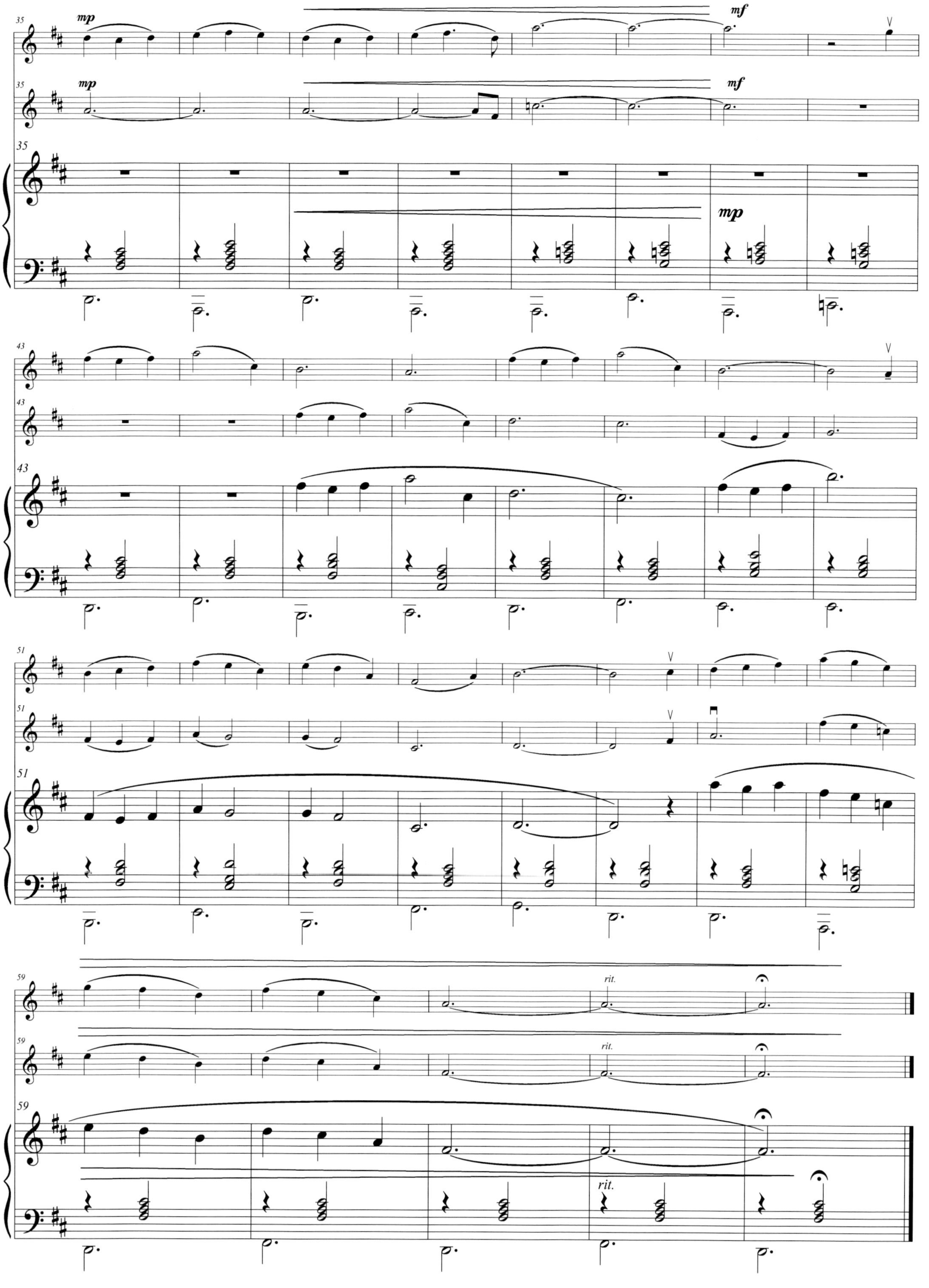
mp
mf
mp
rit.
rit.
rit.

St. Basil's Hymn

Traditional Greek
Arr. Angela Birkhead-Flight

Mystically ♩ = 80

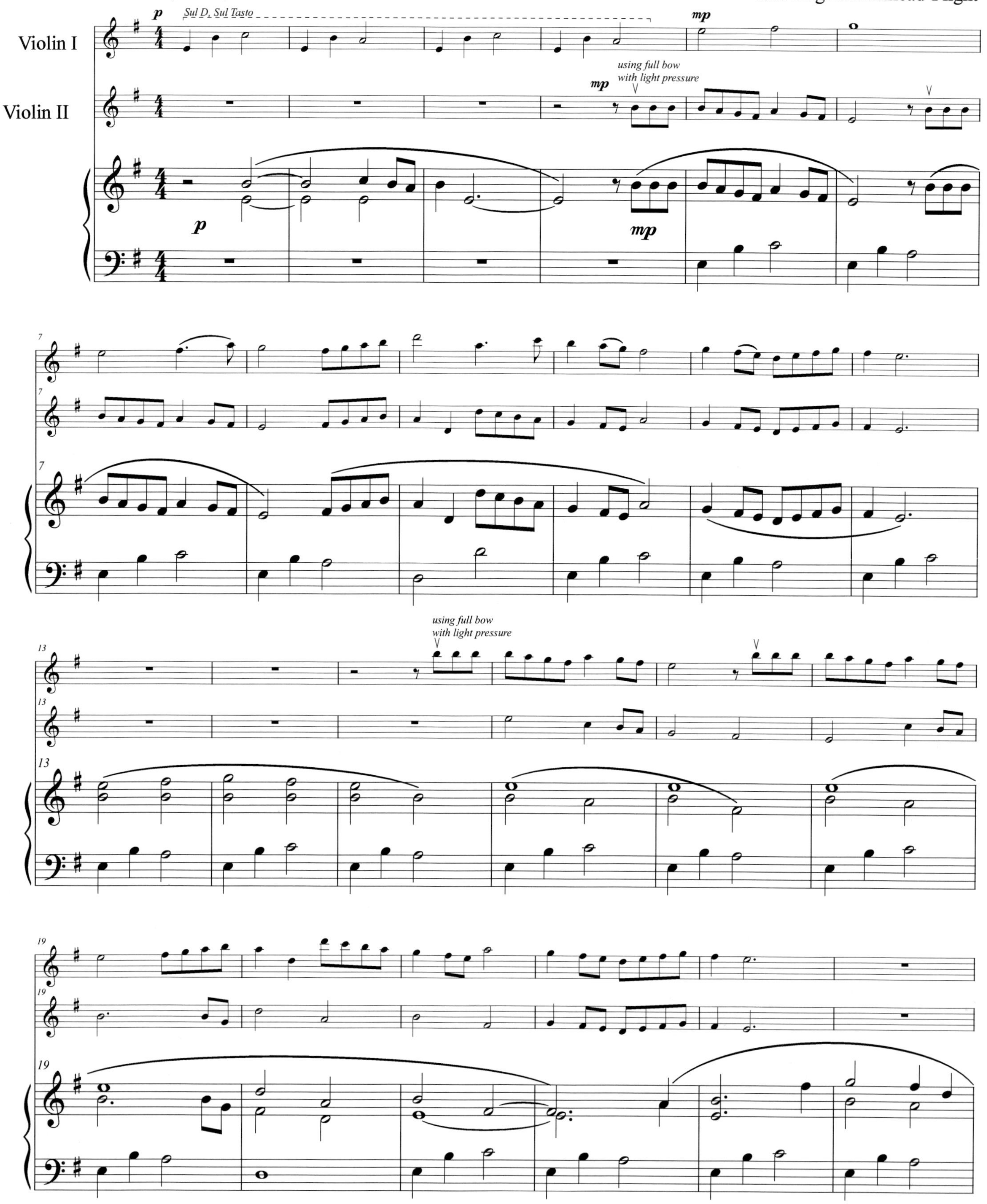

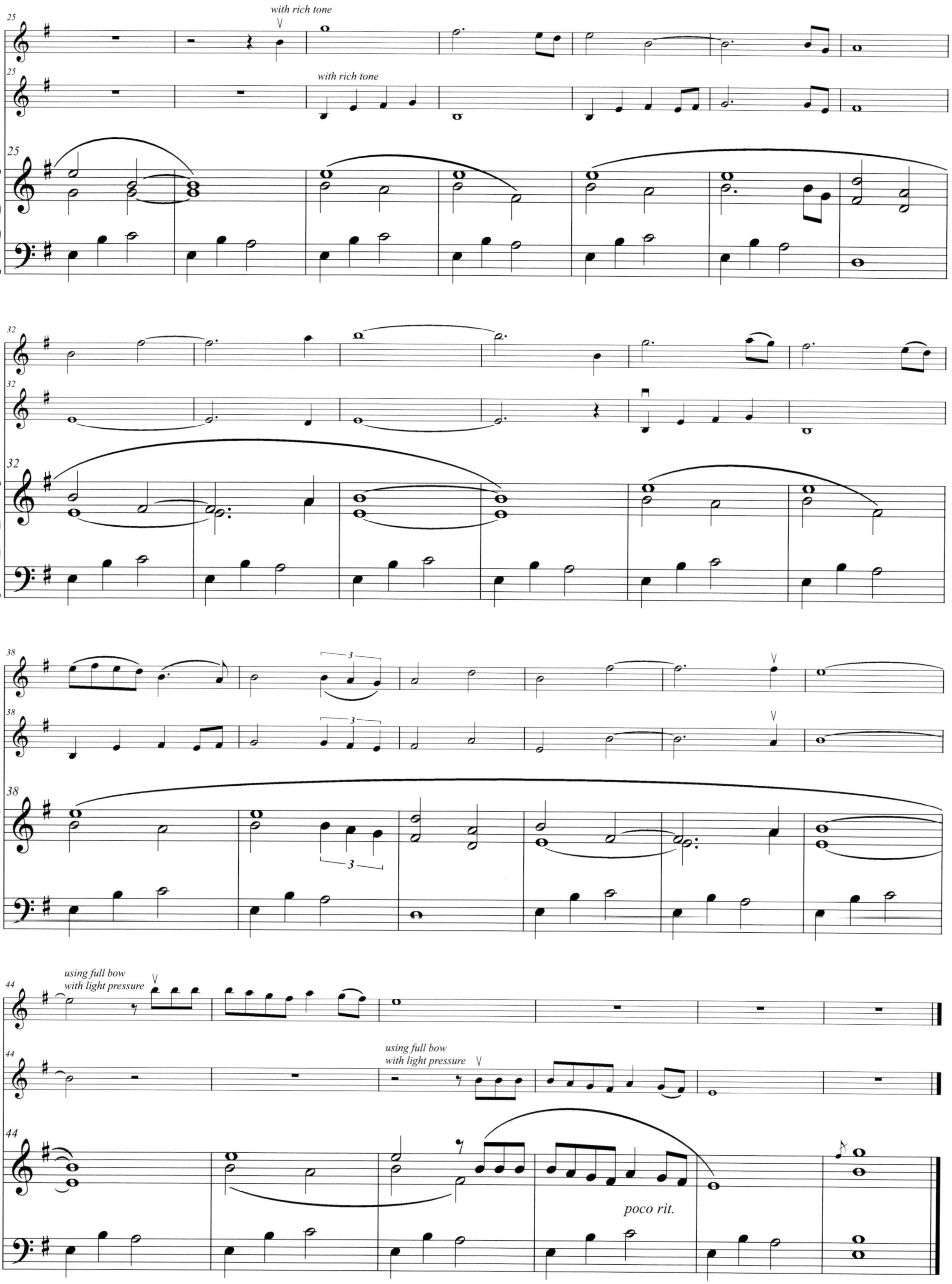
with rich tone
with rich tone
using full bow
with light pressure
using full bow
with light pressure
poco rit.

O Holy Night

Adolphe Adam
Arr. Angela Birkhead-Flight

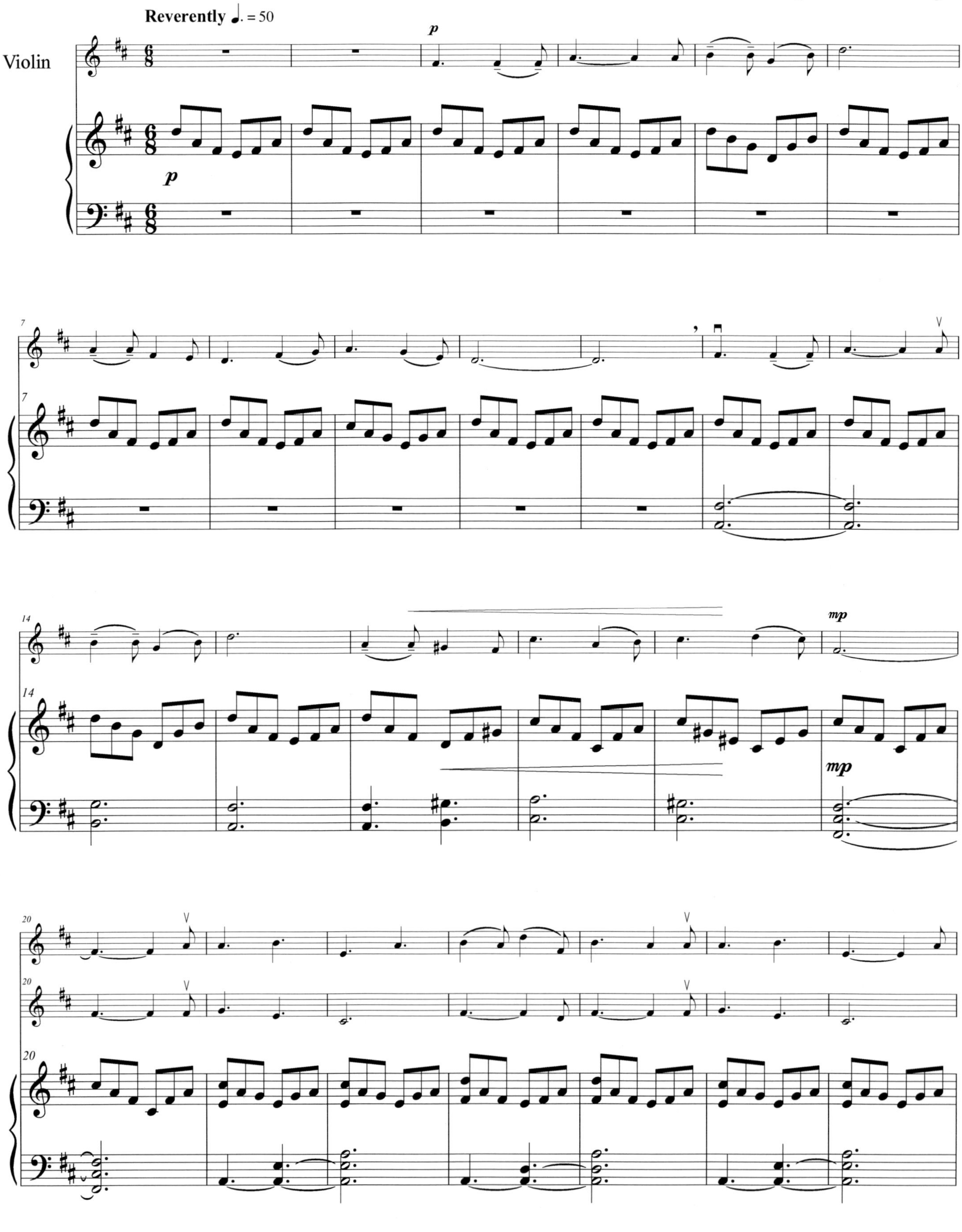

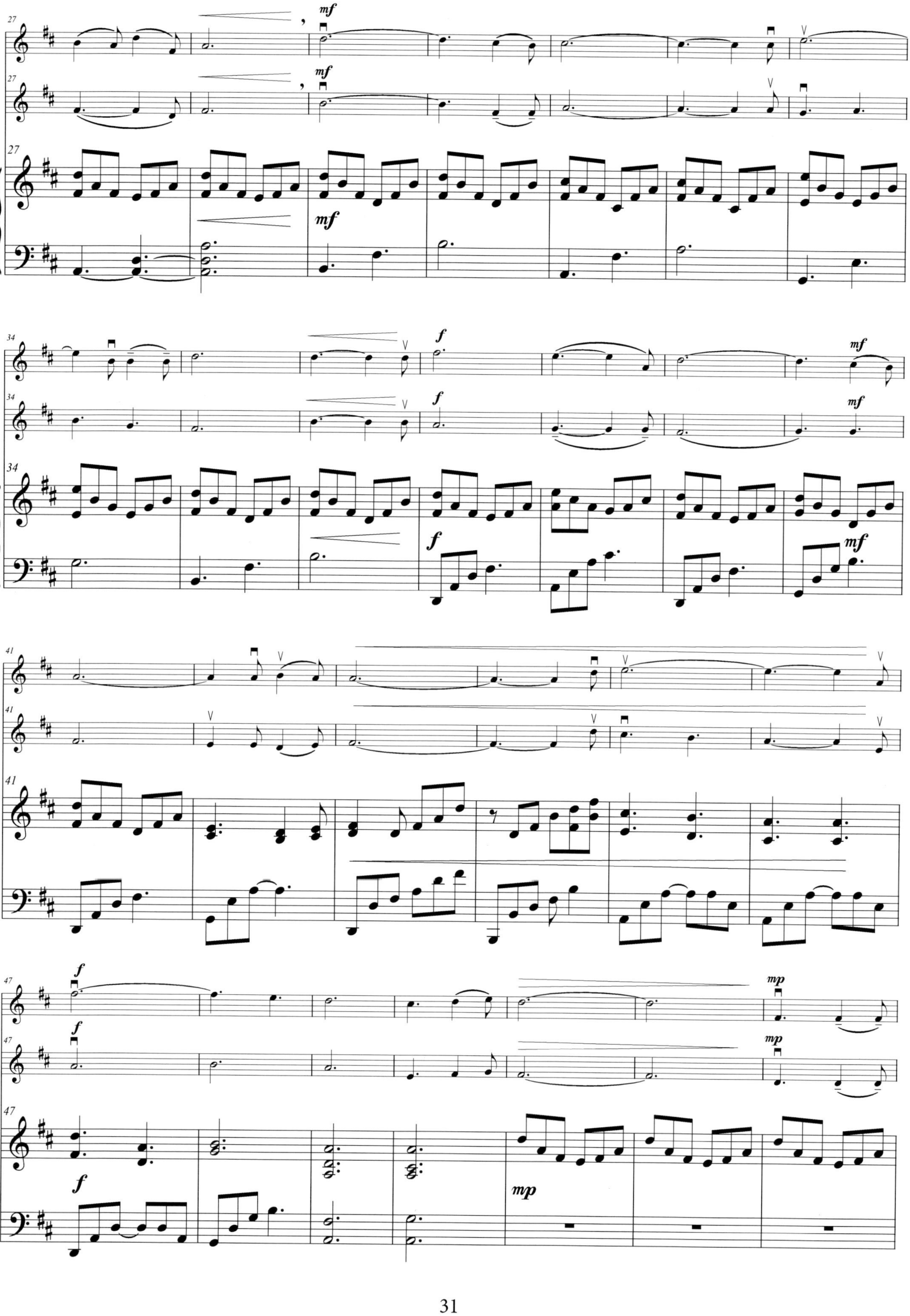

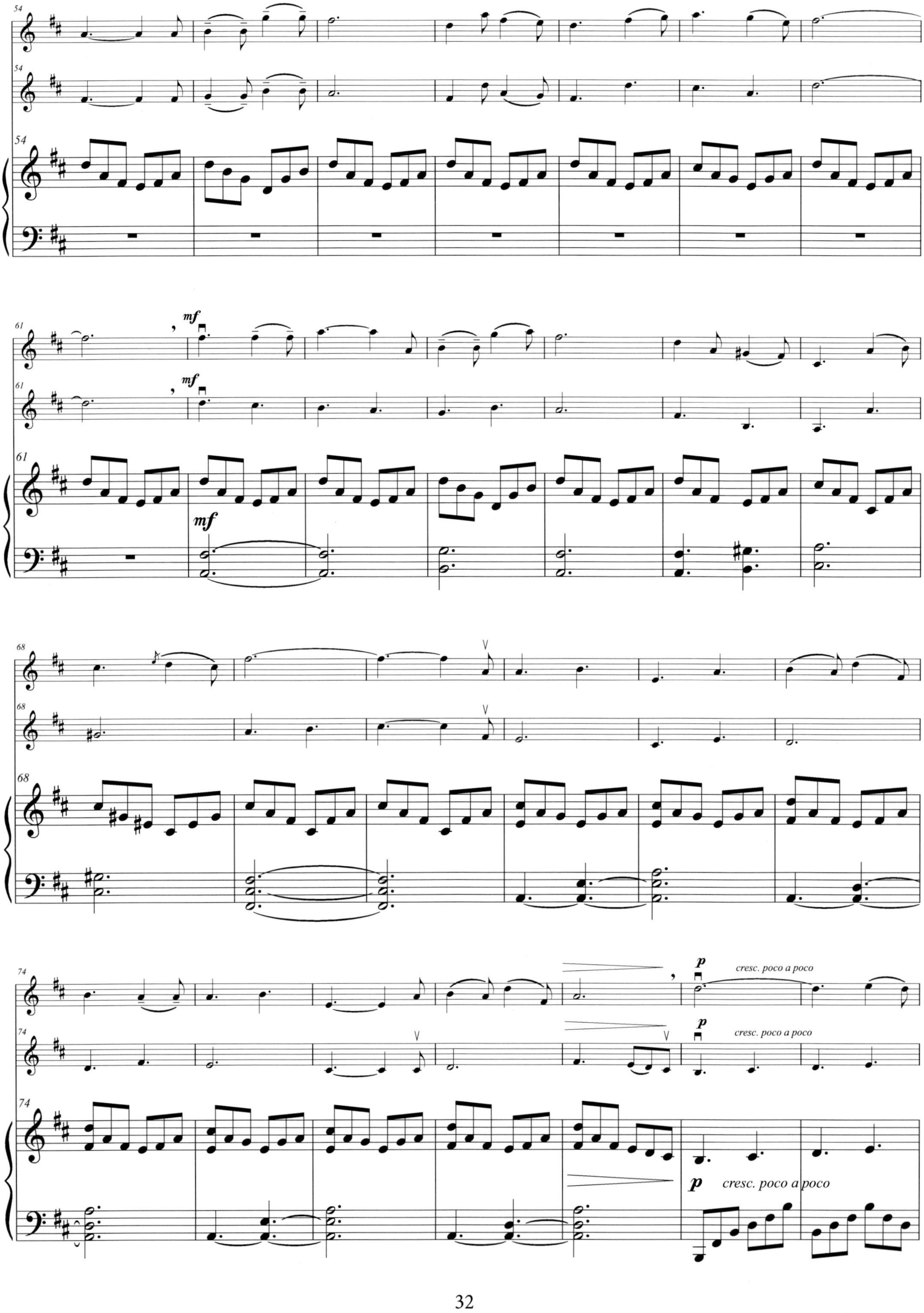
54
61
mf
68
74
p
cresc. poco a poco

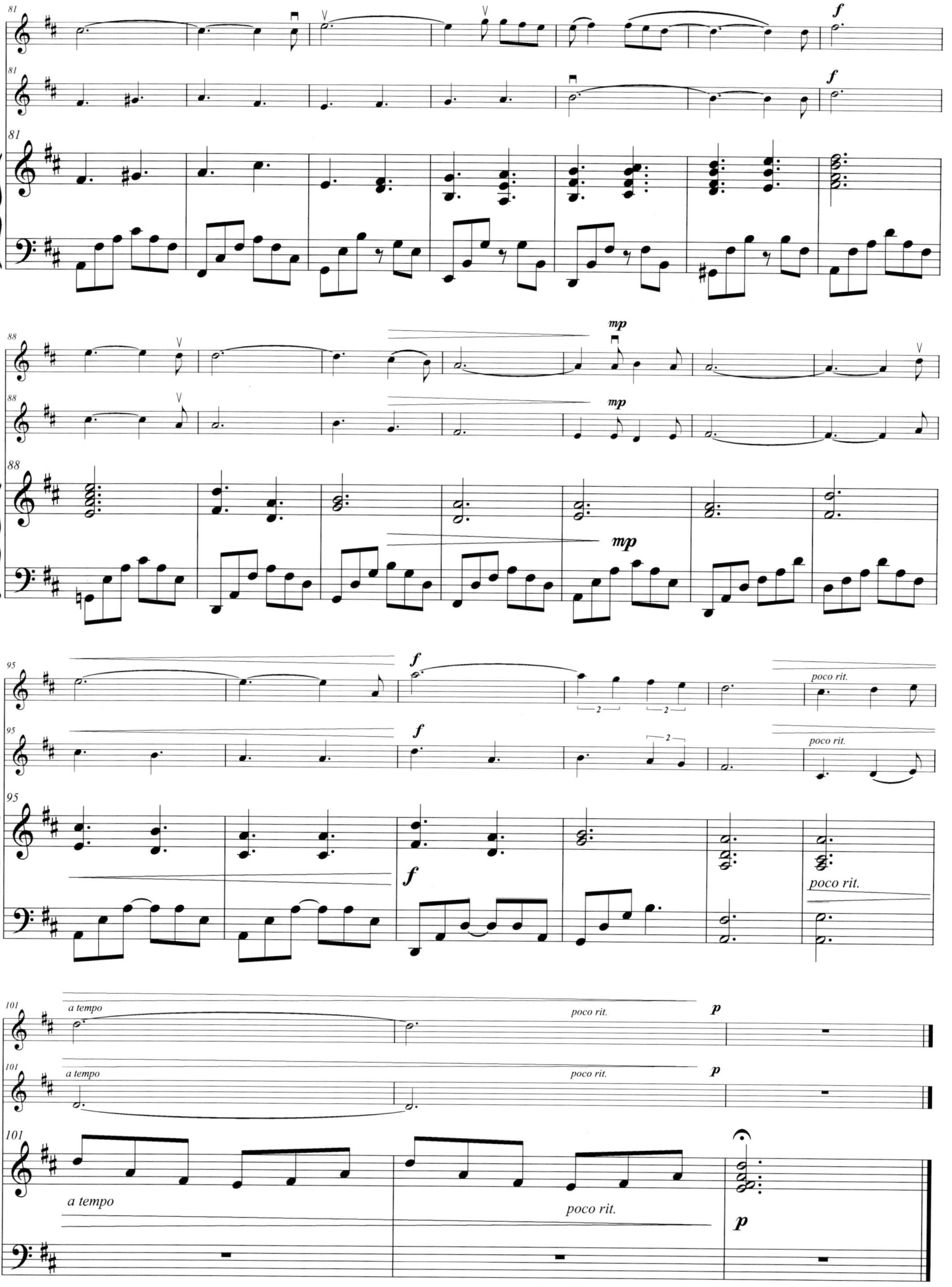
poco rit.
a tempo
poco rit.

What Child Is This?

16th century English melody
Arr. Angela Birkhead-Flight

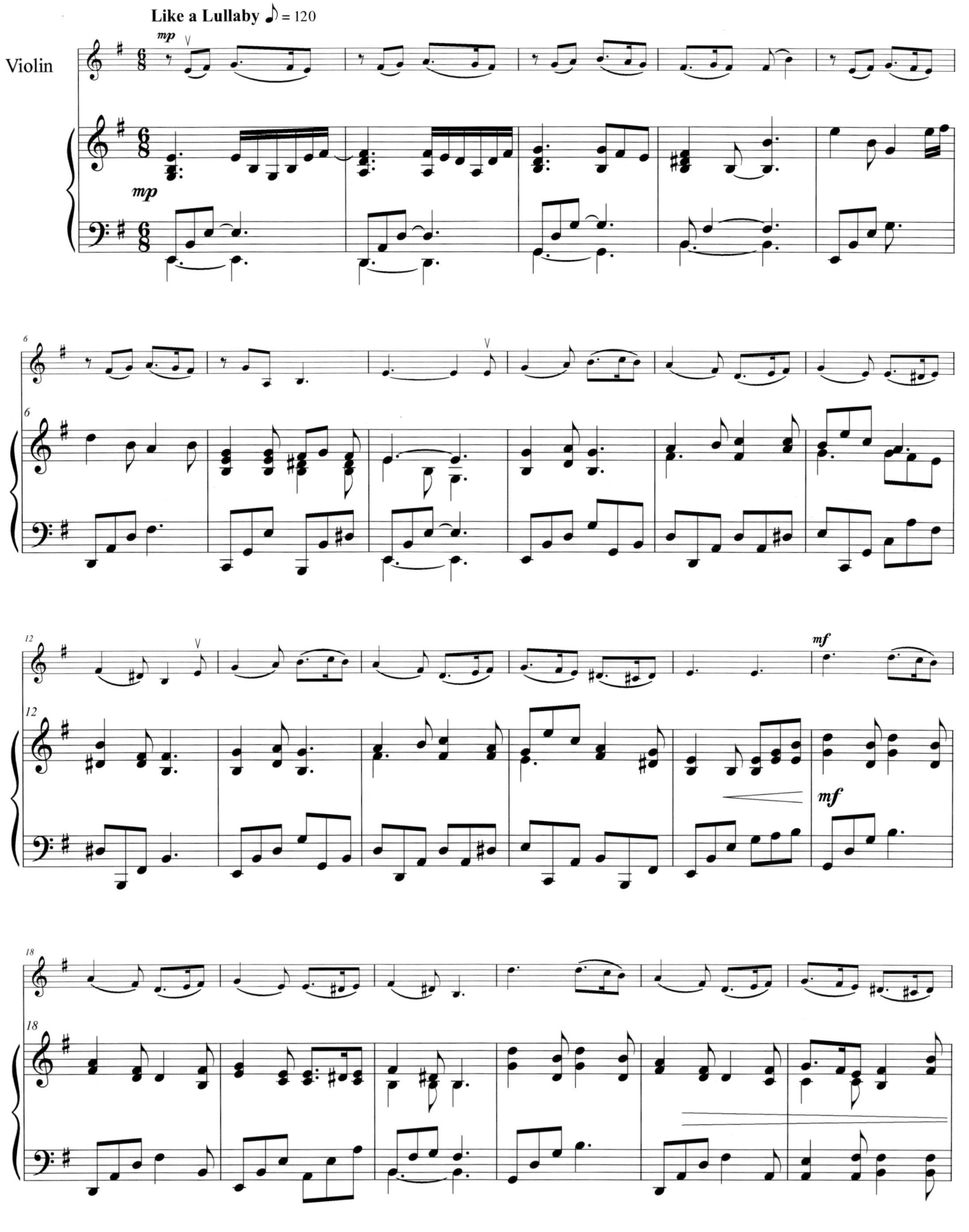

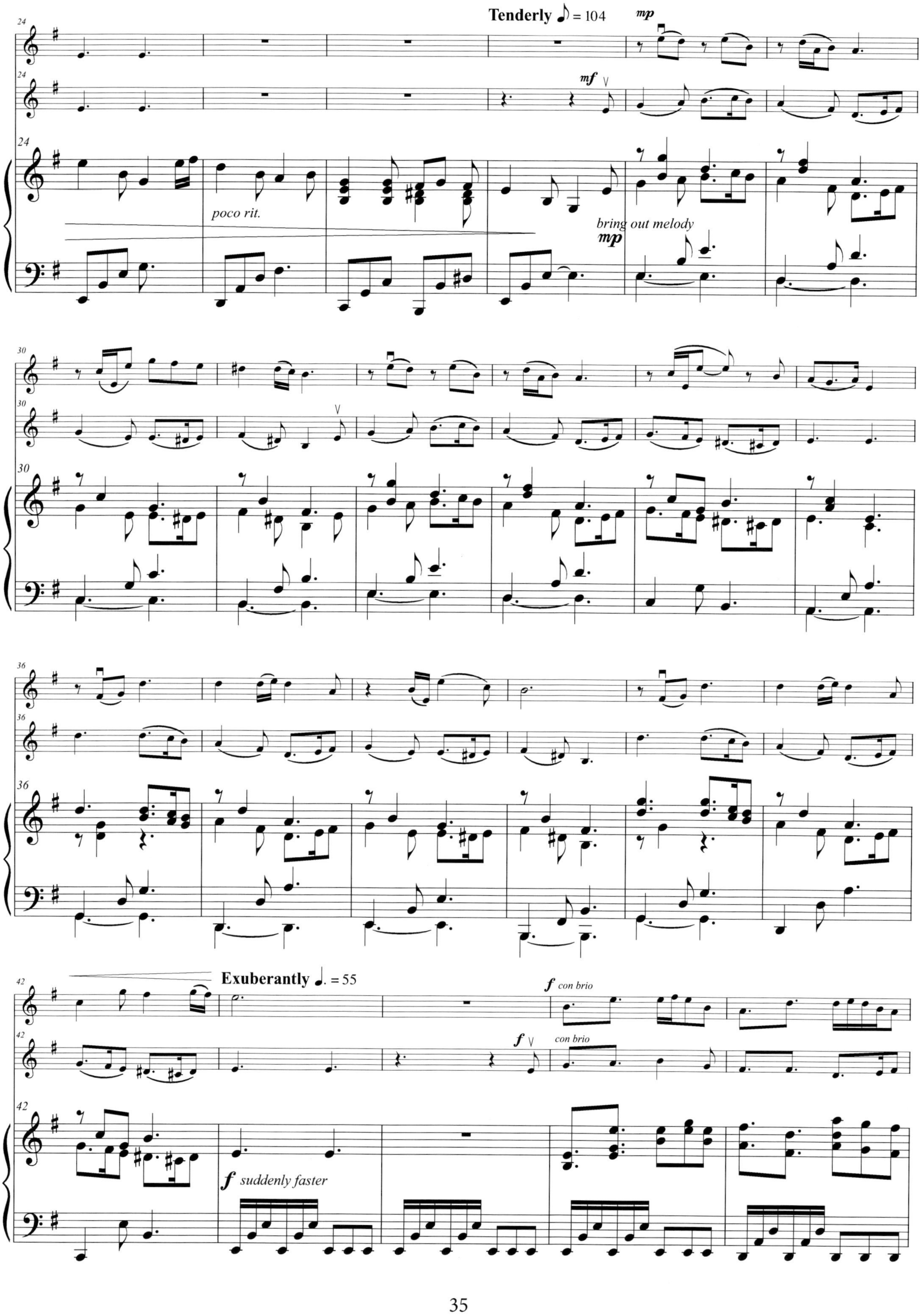

I
II
Tenderly ♪ = 104
poco rit.
bring out melody
Exuberantly ♩. = 55
con brio
suddenly faster

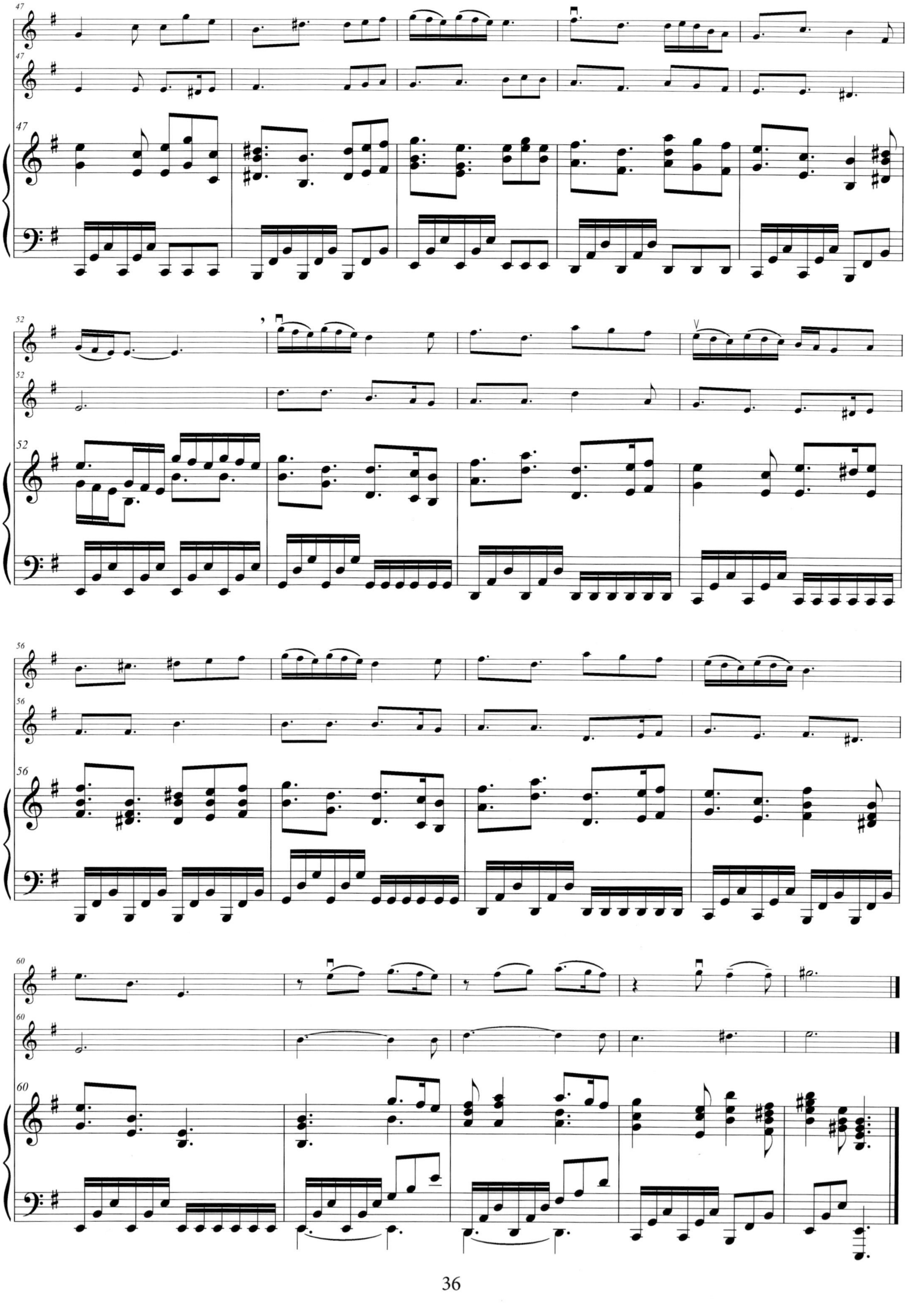

In Concert
Intermediate Violin Solos
or
Duets with Piano
for
Advent, Christmas, and the Holiday Season

by Angela Birkhead-Flight

Violin I

MEL BAY

WWW.MELBAY.COM

Preface

This collection of Advent and Christmas music includes some well-loved classics as well as pieces that will be new discoveries. While both beautiful and fun to play as duets, these pieces can also be performed as solo works using the Violin I part with the piano accompaniment. Each piece goes beyond a straightforward presentation of the main melody to bring a sense of joy and wonder to the music.

Joy to the World / The Ashplant
This exuberant hymn is paired with a snippet of the traditional fiddle tune "The Ashplant," an old-fashioned word for "walking stick." With harmonies winding their way both below and above the main melody, care should be taken to allow the melody to be heard clearly.

O Come, O Come Emmanuel
The light jazz syncopation paired with large dynamic contrasts and soaring improvisatory passages creates a more modern sound for this ancient melody while still conveying a sense of anticipation.

Pat-a-Pan
The crisp quarter note rhythm invoking the drum mentioned in the original lyrics is contrasted with an original lyrical middle section with a soaring melody. This piece has call and answer phrases between the piano and strings that make it a fun collaboration.

Gabriel's Message / Cold Frosty Morning
The 3/4 meter of this mystical, medieval hymn is paired with the toe-tapping 4/4 fiddle tune, invoking the sense of the joy underlying the visit from the angel.

Angels We Have Heard on High
After an introductory pensive verse, this arrangement breaks into a joyful, syncopated collaboration between piano and strings. Followed by a soaring countermelody, there is much opportunity for expression.

Silent Night
The gentle piano part and descending countermelody in the Violin 1 part evoke the gentle falling of snow.

Snowfall
Inspired by Erik Satie's famous work, this piece offers a challenge to the violinist, requiring very controlled bow distribution.

St. Basil's Hymn
Beginning "sul D, sul tasto," this arrangement uses light bow pressure to add to the mysterious nature of this ancient Greek melody. This is contrasted with a section of original music incorporating a richer tone.

O Holy Night

A straight-forward presentation of the hymn is followed by an improvisatory restatement. The dramatic nature of this piece is aided by large dynamic contrasts and a rising scale pattern beneath the main melody.

What Child Is This?

With its sudden shifts in both tempo and mood, this arrangement of "What Child Is This?" reflects the original text of this carol rather than that found in modern hymnals. Beginning as a lullaby, the second verse reflects the pain that is to come ("Nails, spears, shall pierce him through"). A more fiddle-like ending suggests the joy of the epiphany, creating an opportunity to tell a dramatic story with the music.

Angela Birkhead-Flight

Contents

Violin 1

Joy to the World / The Ashplant

"Antioch" by Lowell Mason / Trad. Fiddle Tune
Arr. Angela Birkhead-Flight

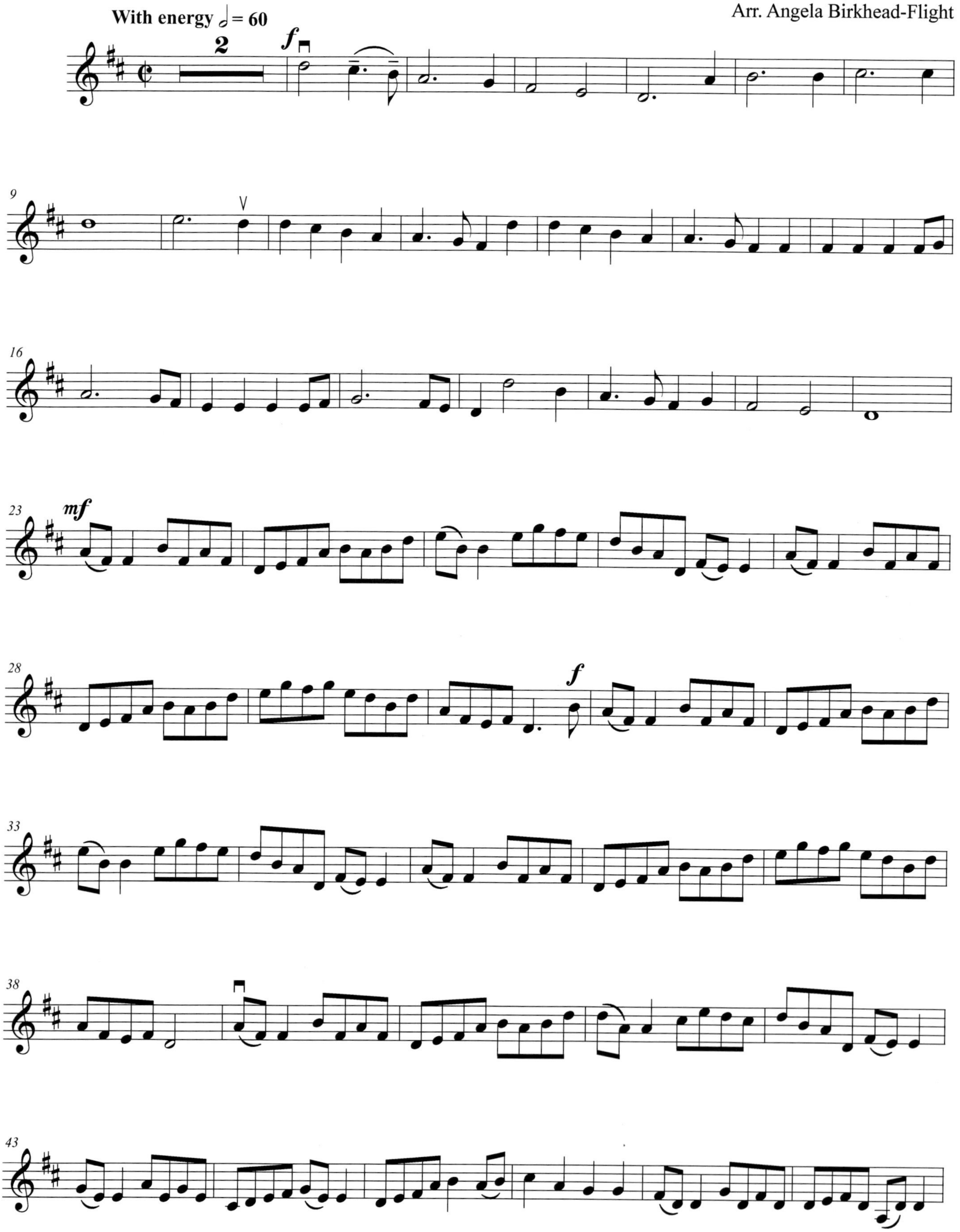

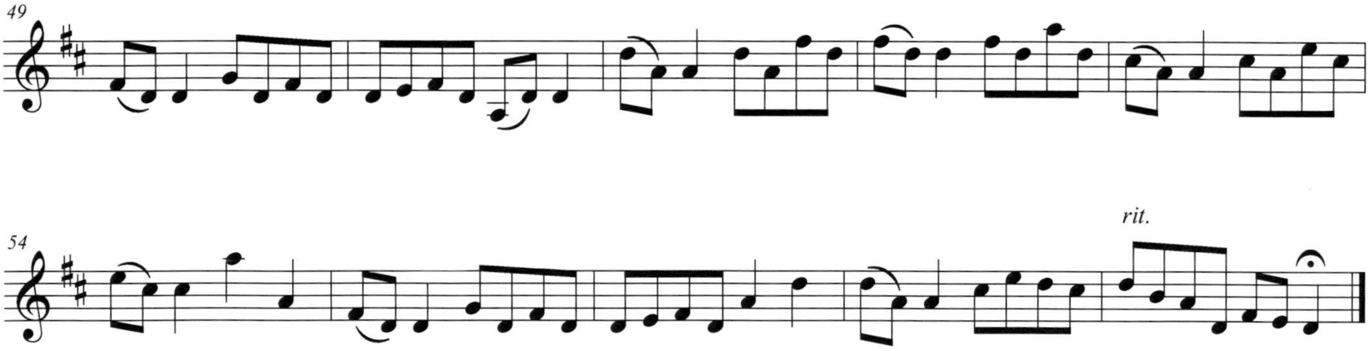
49
54
rit.

Violin 1

O Come, O Come Emmanuel

French, 15th century
Arr. Angela Birkhead-Flight

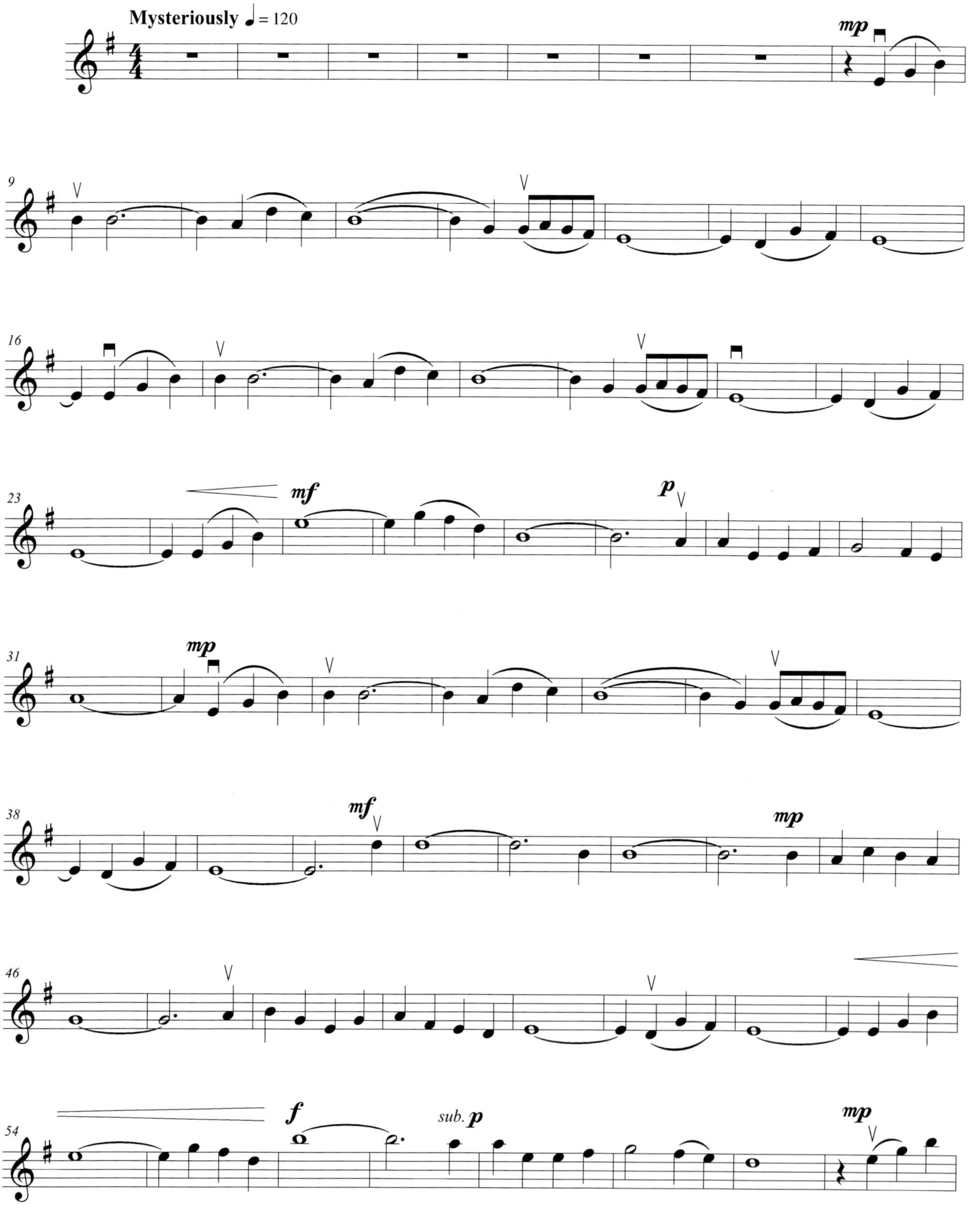

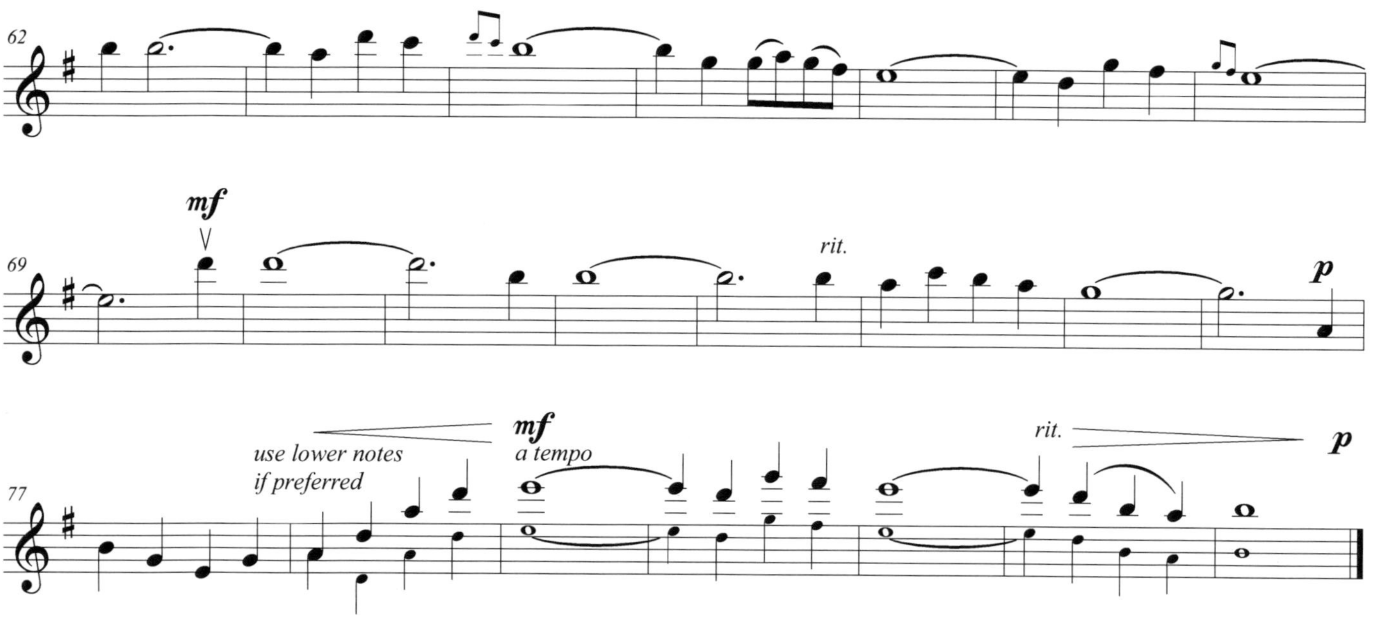
62
69
mf
rit.
p
77
use lower notes
if preferred
mf
a tempo
rit.
p

Violin 1

Pat-a-Pan

Bernard de La Monnoye (1641–1728)
Arr. Angela Birkhead-Flight

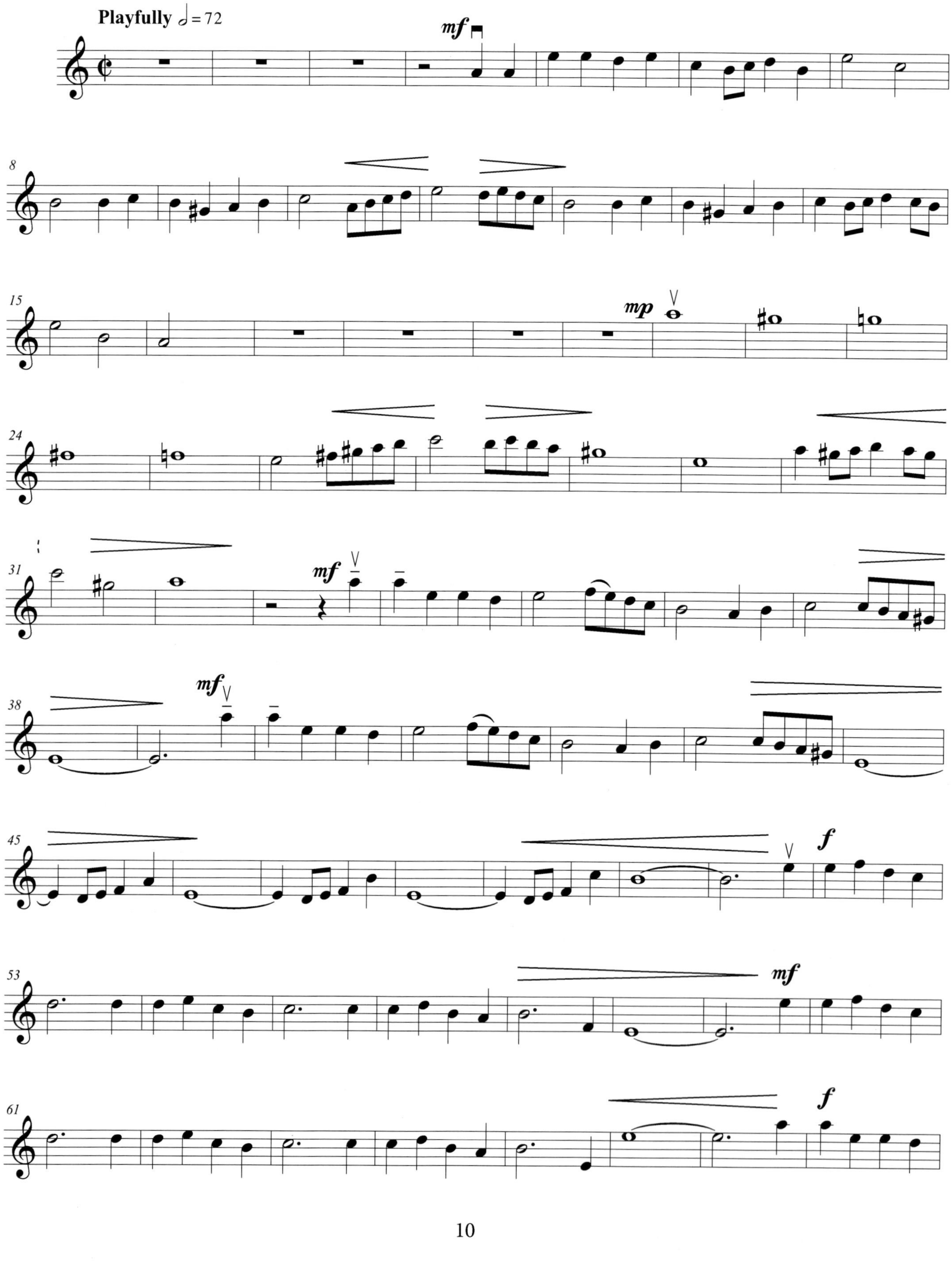

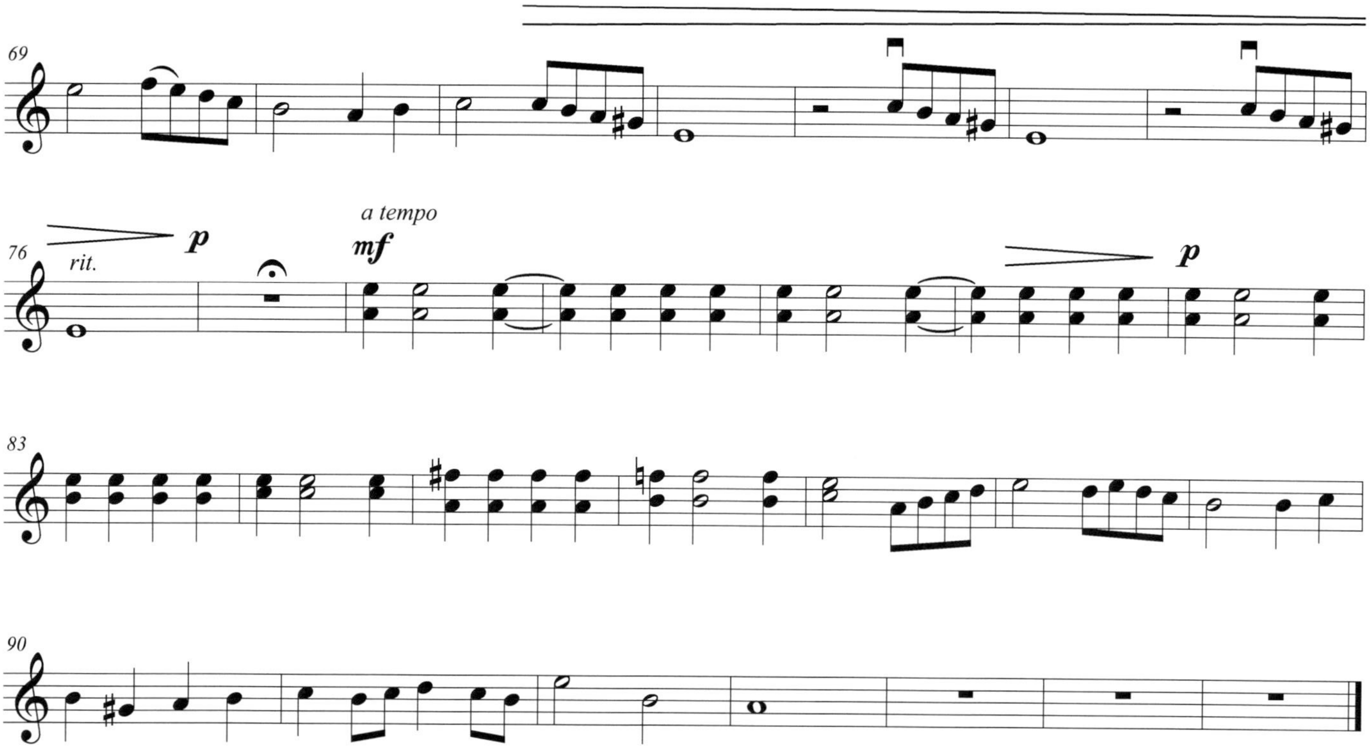
rit.
a tempo
mf
p

Gabriel's Message / Cold Frosty Morning

Basque Folk Carol / American Fiddle Tune
Arr. Angela Birkhead-Flight

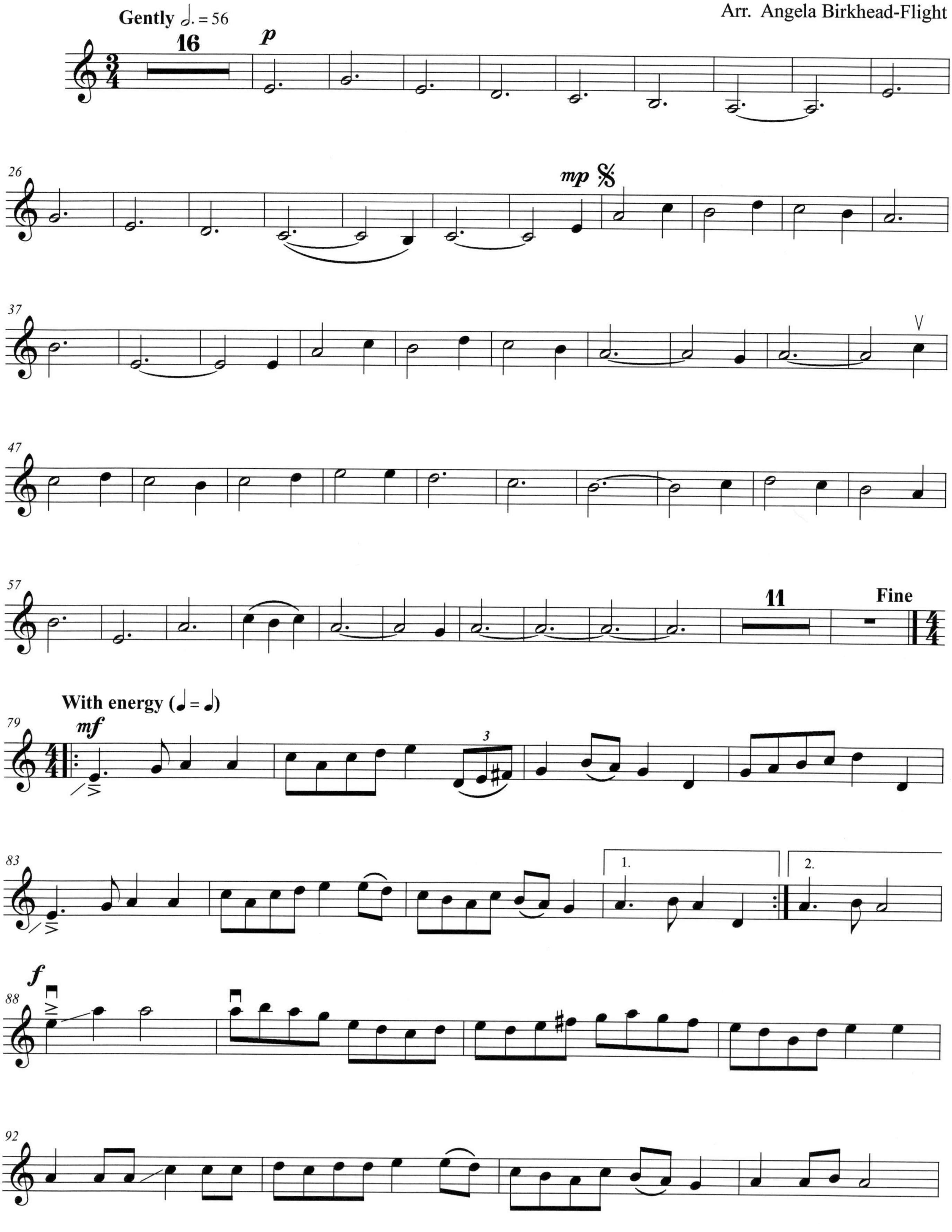

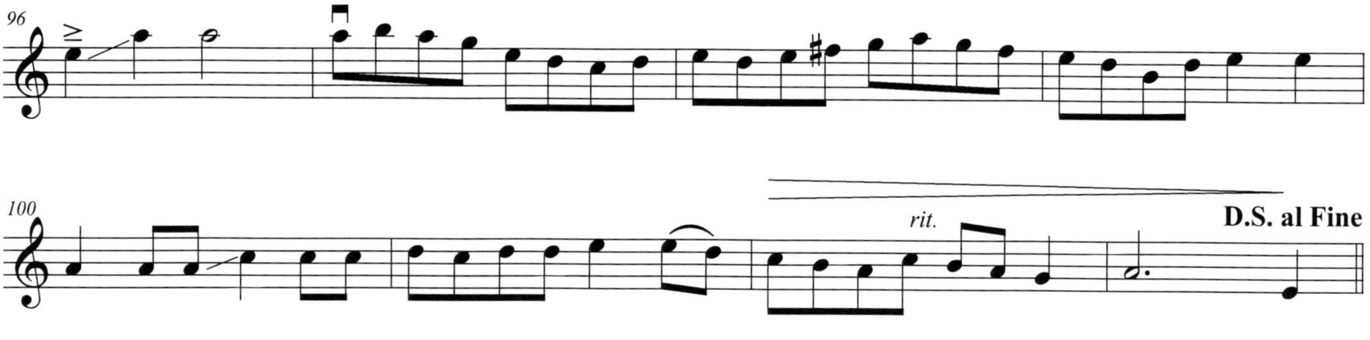
96
100
rit.
D.S. al Fine

Violin 1

Angels We Have Heard on High

Traditional French Carol
Arr. Angela Birkhead-Flight

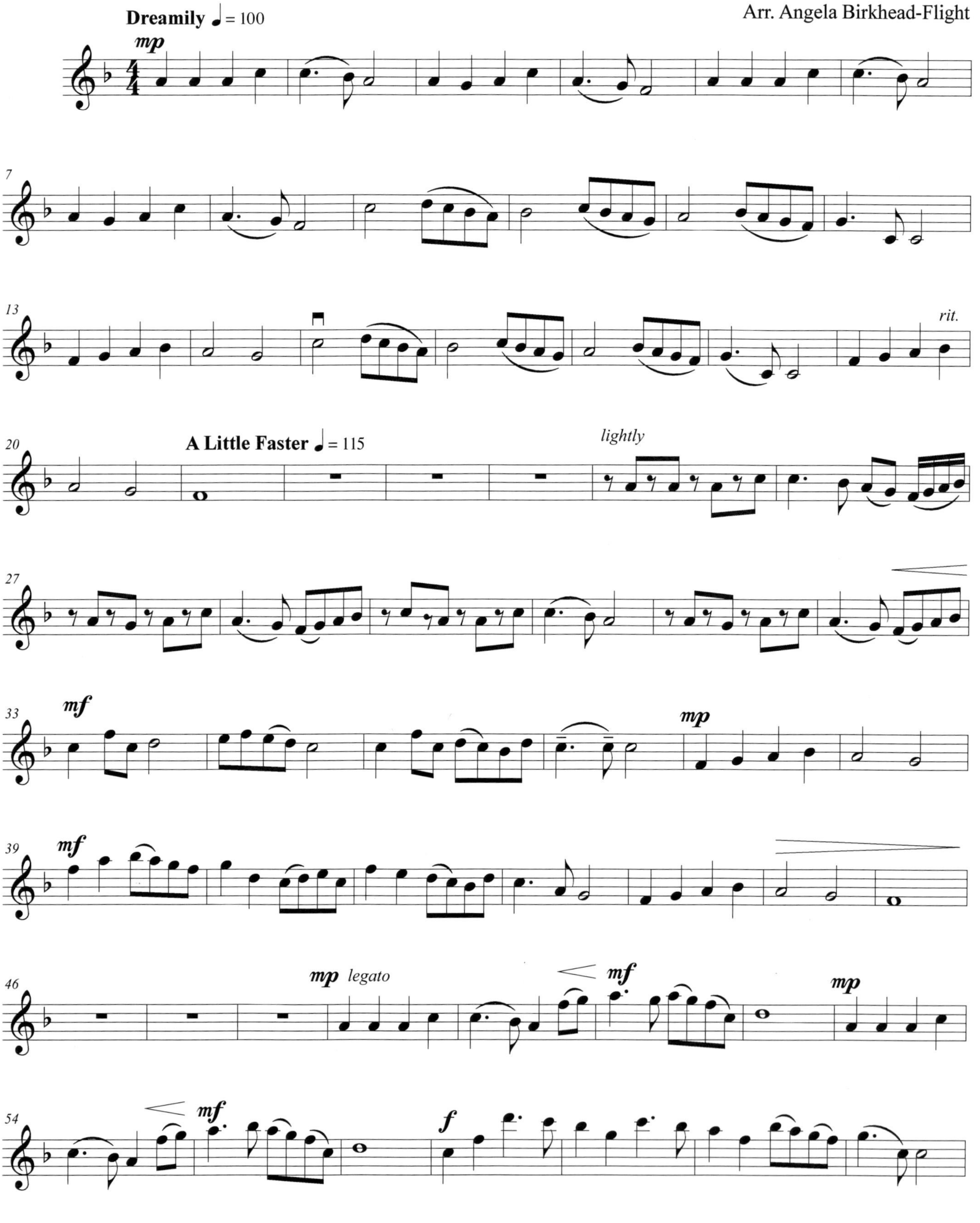

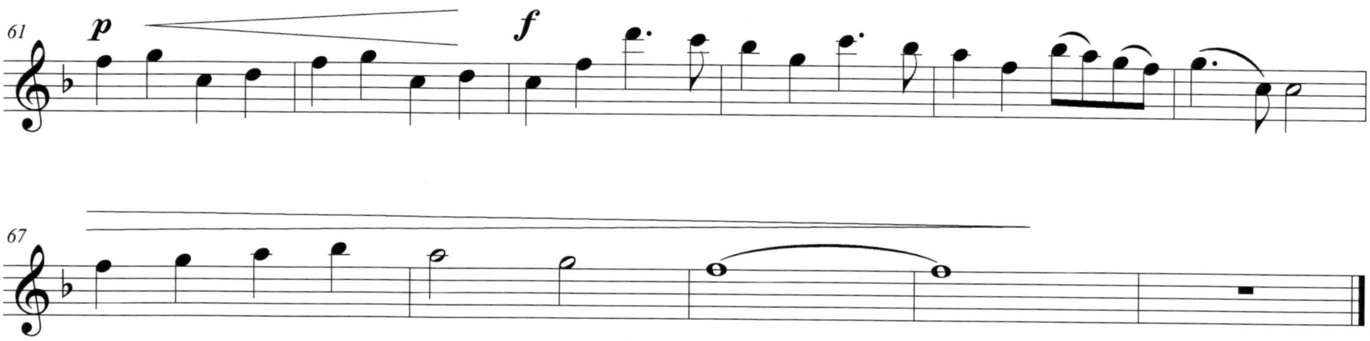
61
p
f
67

Violin 1

Silent Night

Franz Gruber
Arr. Angela Birkhead-Flight

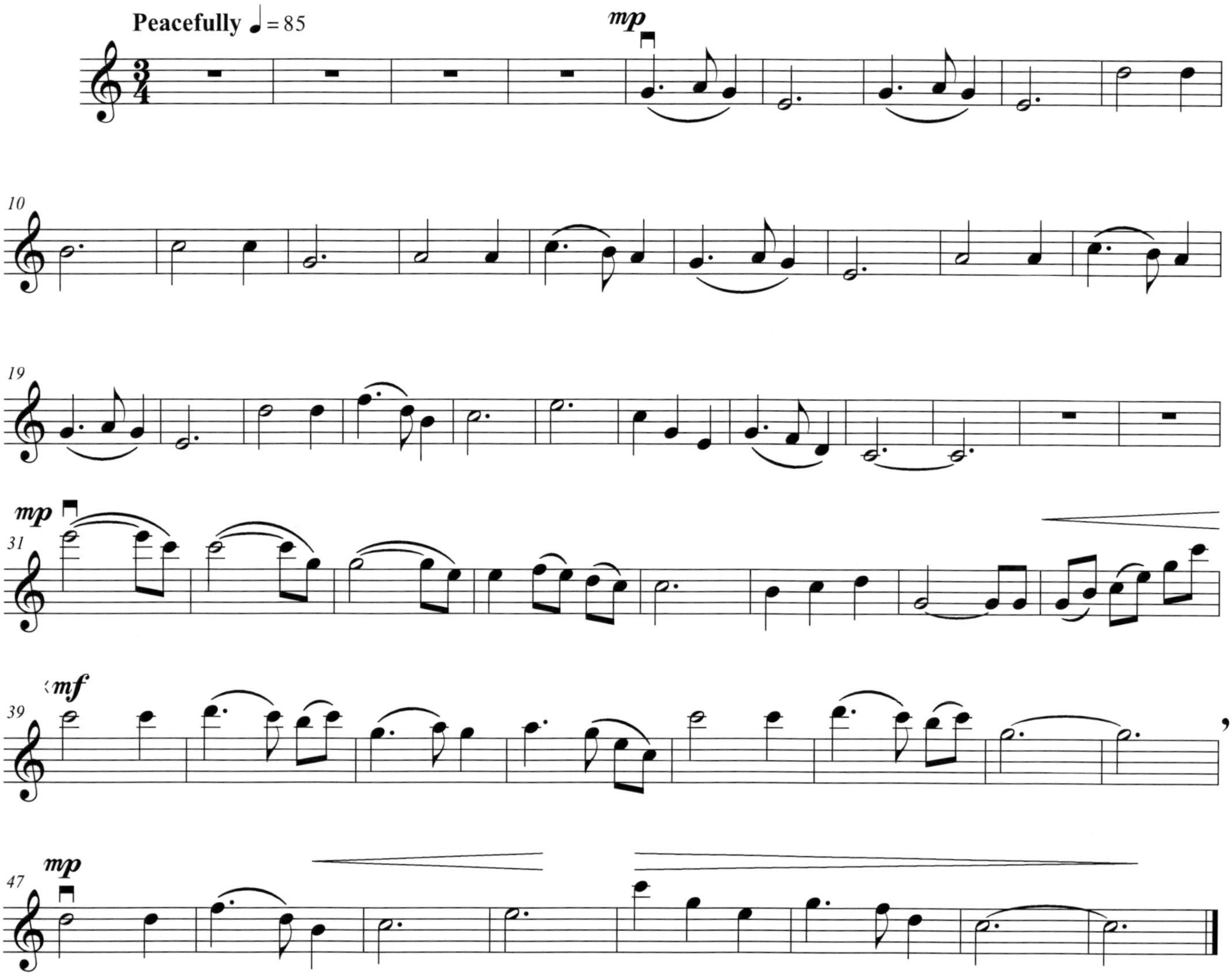

Violin 1

Snowfall

Inspired by Gymnopédie No. 1
by Erik Satie
Angela Birkhead-Flight

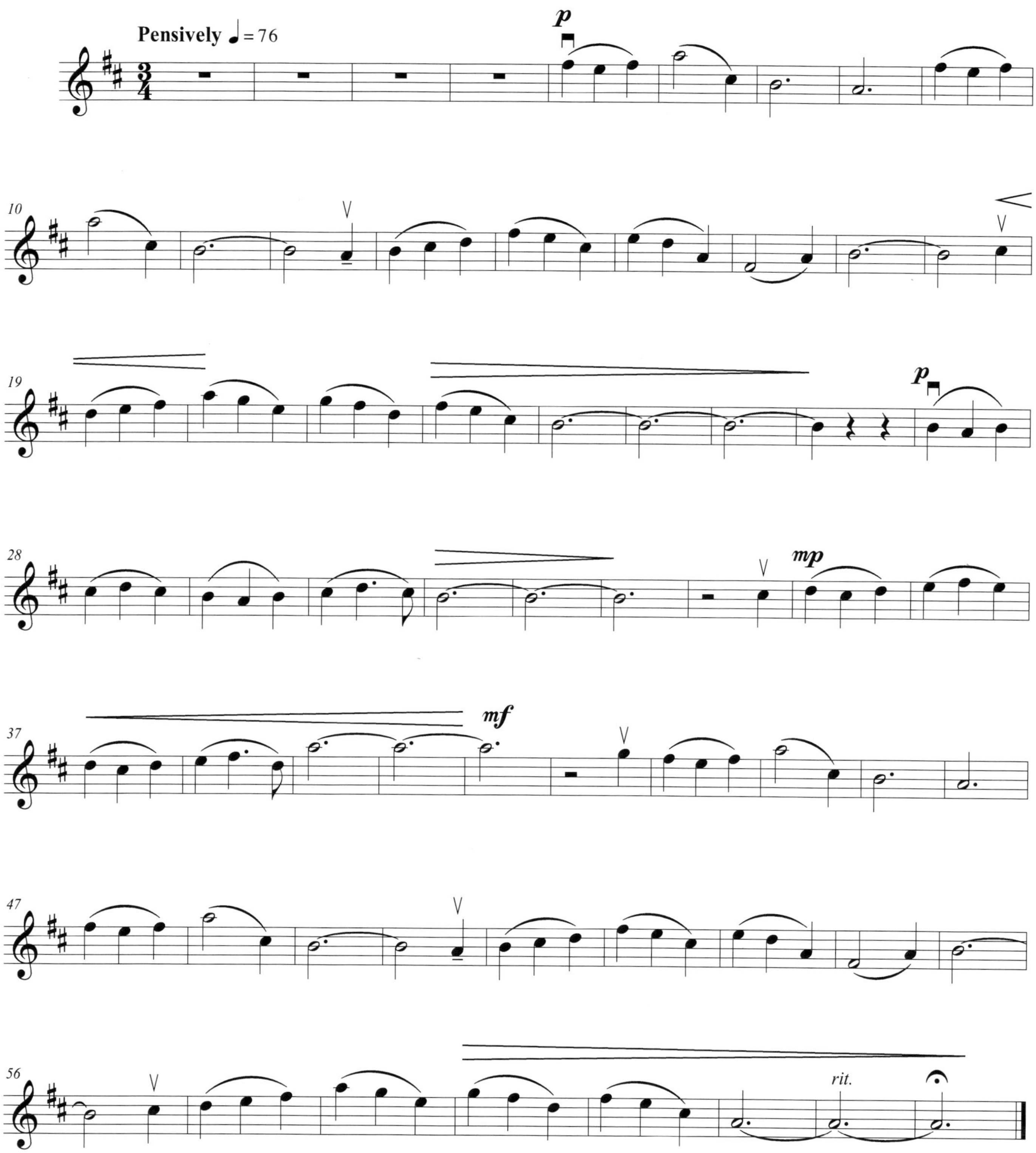

Violin 1

St. Basil's Hymn

Traditional Greek
Arr. Angela Birkhead-Flight

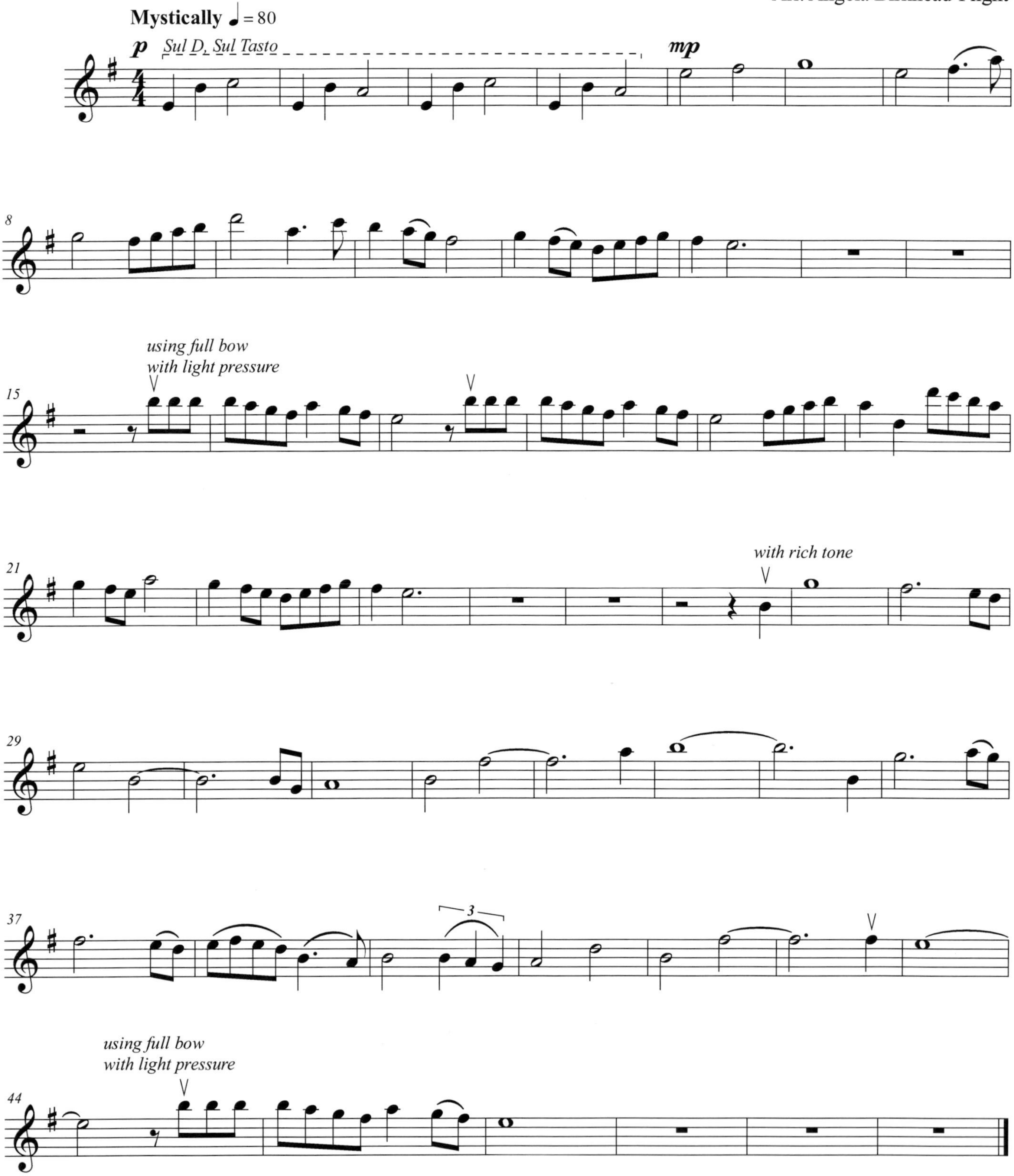

This page has been left blank to avoid an awkward page turn.

Violin 1

O Holy Night

Adolphe Adam
Arr. Angela Birkhead-Flight

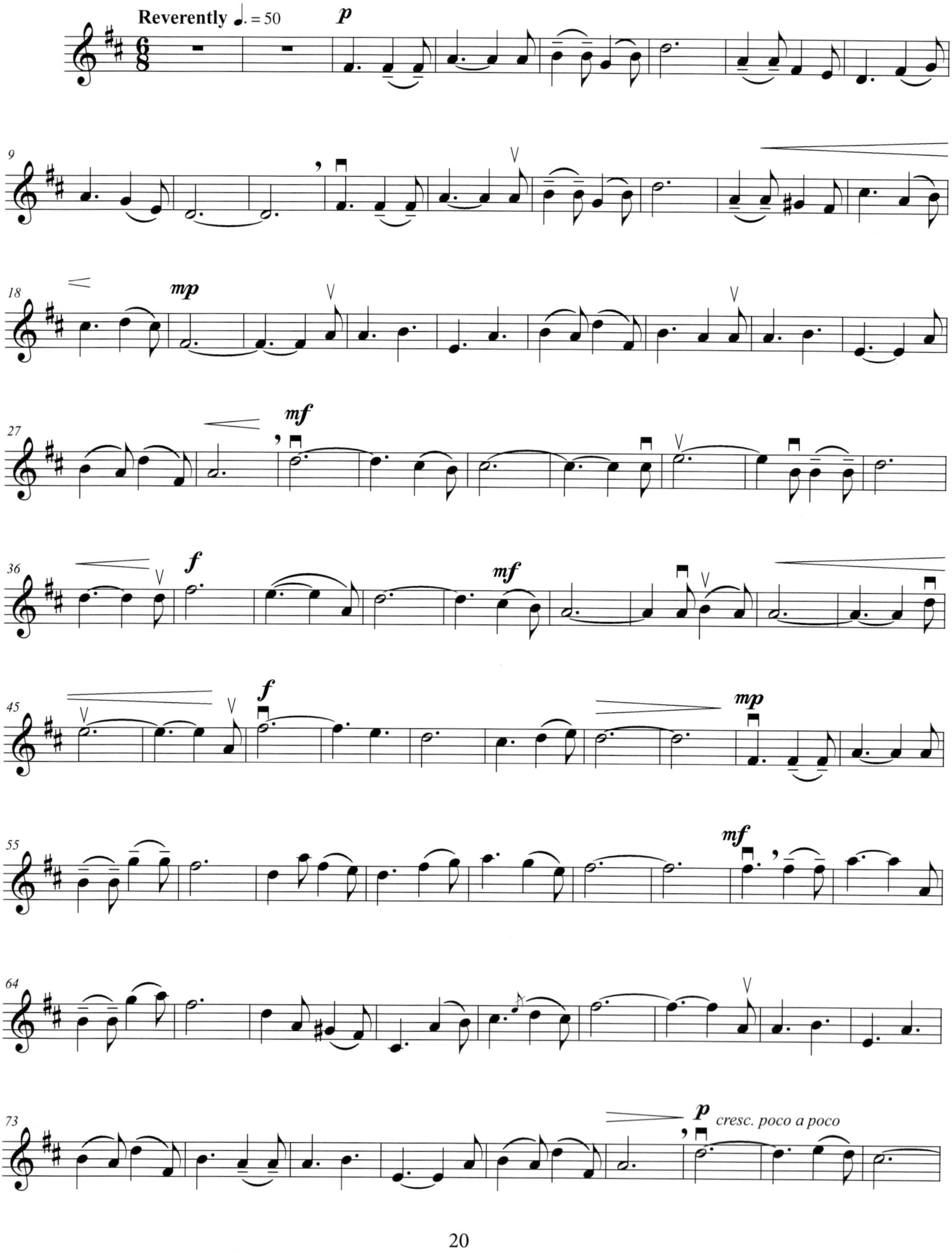

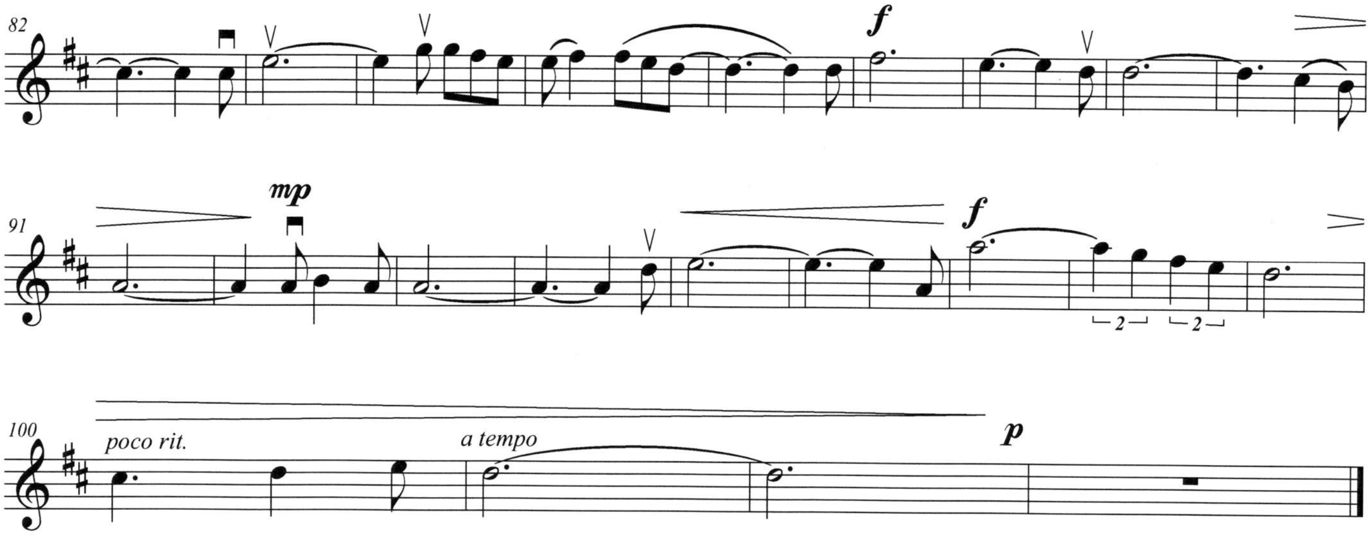
82
f
91
mp
f
100
poco rit.
a tempo
p

Violin 1

What Child Is This?

16th century English melody
Arr. Angela Birkhead-Flight

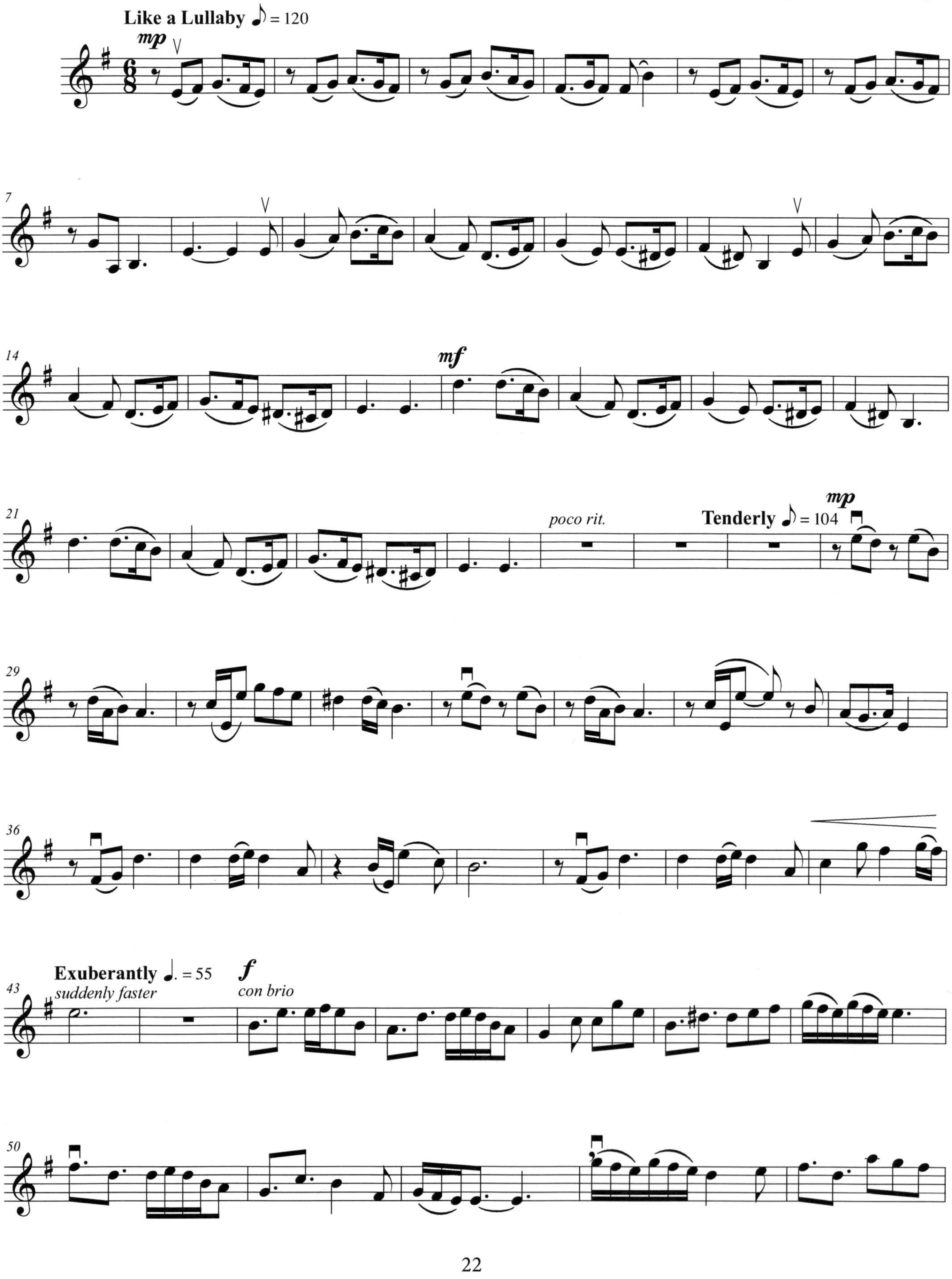

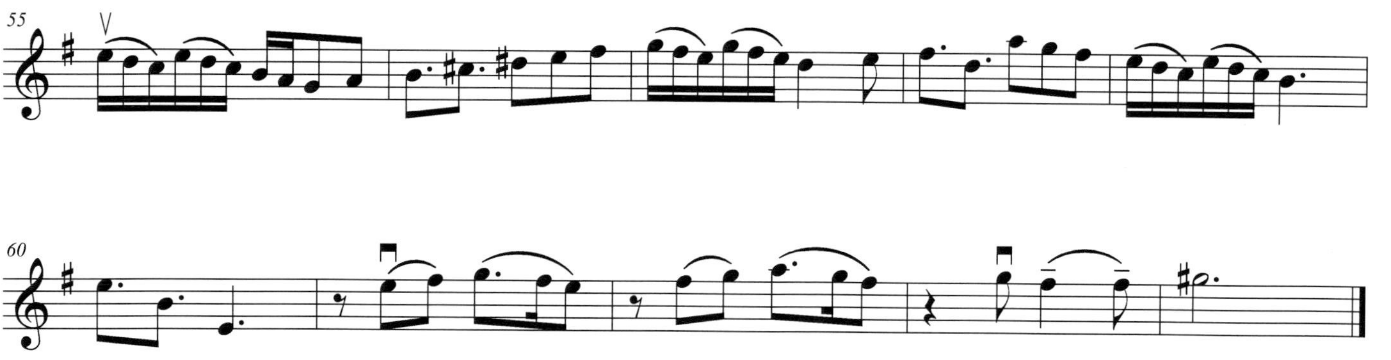

Other Mel Bay Violin Duet and Ensemble Books

American Fiddle Tunes for Solo & Ensemble: Violins 1 & 2 (C. Duncan)

American Fiddle Tunes for Solo & Ensemble: Viola, Violin 3 & Ensemble Score (C. Duncan)

Beautiful Melodies from Around the World -For Two Violins (Cooper)

Celtic Fiddle Tunes for Solo & Ensemble: Violins 1 & 2 (C. Duncan)

Celtic Fiddle Tunes for Solo & Ensemble:: Viola, Violin 3 & Ensemble Score (C. Duncan)

Christmas Music Arranged for Violin Duet (Staidle)

Christmas Strings: Violin 1 & 2 with Piano Accompaniment (Miller)

Christmas Strings: Viola/Violin 3 & Ensemble Score (Miller)

Come Fiddle with Me Volume 1 - Duets (Hay)

Come Fiddle with Me Volume 2 - Duets (Hay)

Eastern European Music for Violin Duet (Harbar)

Easy Duets for Violin (Puscoiu)

Easy Violin Duets in First Position (Isaac)

Fiddling Classics for Solo & Ensemble: Violins 1 & 2 (C. Duncan)

Fiddling Classics for Solo & Ensemble: Viola, Violin 3 & Ensemble Score (C. Duncan

First Lessons Violin Duets (C. Duncan)

J. S. Bach: Duets for Two Violins (Spencer/Engle)

Jazz Duets: Violin Edition (Biondi)

Music from Around the World for Solo & Ensemble: Violins 1 & 2 (Miller)

Music from Around the World for Solo & Ensemble: Viola/Violin 3 (Miller)

My Very Best Christmas-Violin Edition (Khanagov)

Ragtimes for Two Violins (Brydern)

Scottish Airs and Dances for Violin Solo or Duet (Witt)

Scottish Melodies for Violin Solo or Duet (Witt)

Traditional Hymns for Violin Solo or Duet (Khanagov)

Twin Fiddling (Phillips)

Violin Duet Classics Made Playable (Harbar)

Wedding Music for String Quartet (Staidle)

Wedding Music for Two Violins (Staidle)

Wedding Music for Violin and Viola (Staidle)

Winter-Violin & Cello (Parks & Groschang)

In Concert

Intermediate Violin Solos
or
Duets with Piano
for
Advent, Christmas, and the Holiday Season

by Angela Birkhead-Flight

Violin II

WWW.MELBAY.COM

Preface

This collection of Advent and Christmas music includes some well-loved classics as well as pieces that will be new discoveries. While both beautiful and fun to play as duets, these pieces can also be performed as solo works using the Violin I part with the piano accompaniment. Each piece goes beyond a straightforward presentation of the main melody to bring a sense of joy and wonder to the music.

Joy to the World / The Ashplant
This exuberant hymn is paired with a snippet of the traditional fiddle tune "The Ashplant," an old-fashioned word for "walking stick." With harmonies winding their way both below and above the main melody, care should be taken to allow the melody to be heard clearly.

O Come, O Come Emmanuel
The light jazz syncopation paired with large dynamic contrasts and soaring improvisatory passages creates a more modern sound for this ancient melody while still conveying a sense of anticipation.

Pat-a-Pan
The crisp quarter note rhythm invoking the drum mentioned in the original lyrics is contrasted with an original lyrical middle section with a soaring melody. This piece has call and answer phrases between the piano and strings that make it a fun collaboration.

Gabriel's Message / Cold Frosty Morning
The 3/4 meter of this mystical, medieval hymn is paired with the toe-tapping 4/4 fiddle tune, invoking the sense of the joy underlying the visit from the angel.

Angels We Have Heard on High
After an introductory pensive verse, this arrangement breaks into a joyful, syncopated collaboration between piano and strings. Followed by a soaring countermelody, there is much opportunity for expression.

Silent Night
The gentle piano part and descending countermelody in the Violin 1 part evoke the gentle falling of snow.

Snowfall
Inspired by Erik Satie's famous work, this piece offers a challenge to the violinist, requiring very controlled bow distribution.

St. Basil's Hymn
Beginning "sul D, sul tasto," this arrangement uses light bow pressure to add to the mysterious nature of this ancient Greek melody. This is contrasted with a section of original music incorporating a richer tone.

O Holy Night
A straight-forward presentation of the hymn is followed by an improvisatory restatement. The dramatic nature of this piece is aided by large dynamic contrasts and a rising scale pattern beneath the main melody.

What Child Is This?
With its sudden shifts in both tempo and mood, this arrangement of "What Child Is This?" reflects the original text of this carol rather than that found in modern hymnals. Beginning as a lullaby, the second verse reflects the pain that is to come ("Nails, spears, shall pierce him through"). A more fiddle-like ending suggests the joy of the epiphany, creating an opportunity to tell a dramatic story with the music.

Angela Birkhead-Flight

Contents

Violin 2

Joy to the World / The Ashplant

"Antioch" by Lowell Mason / Trad. Fiddle Tune
Arr. Angela Birkhead-Flight

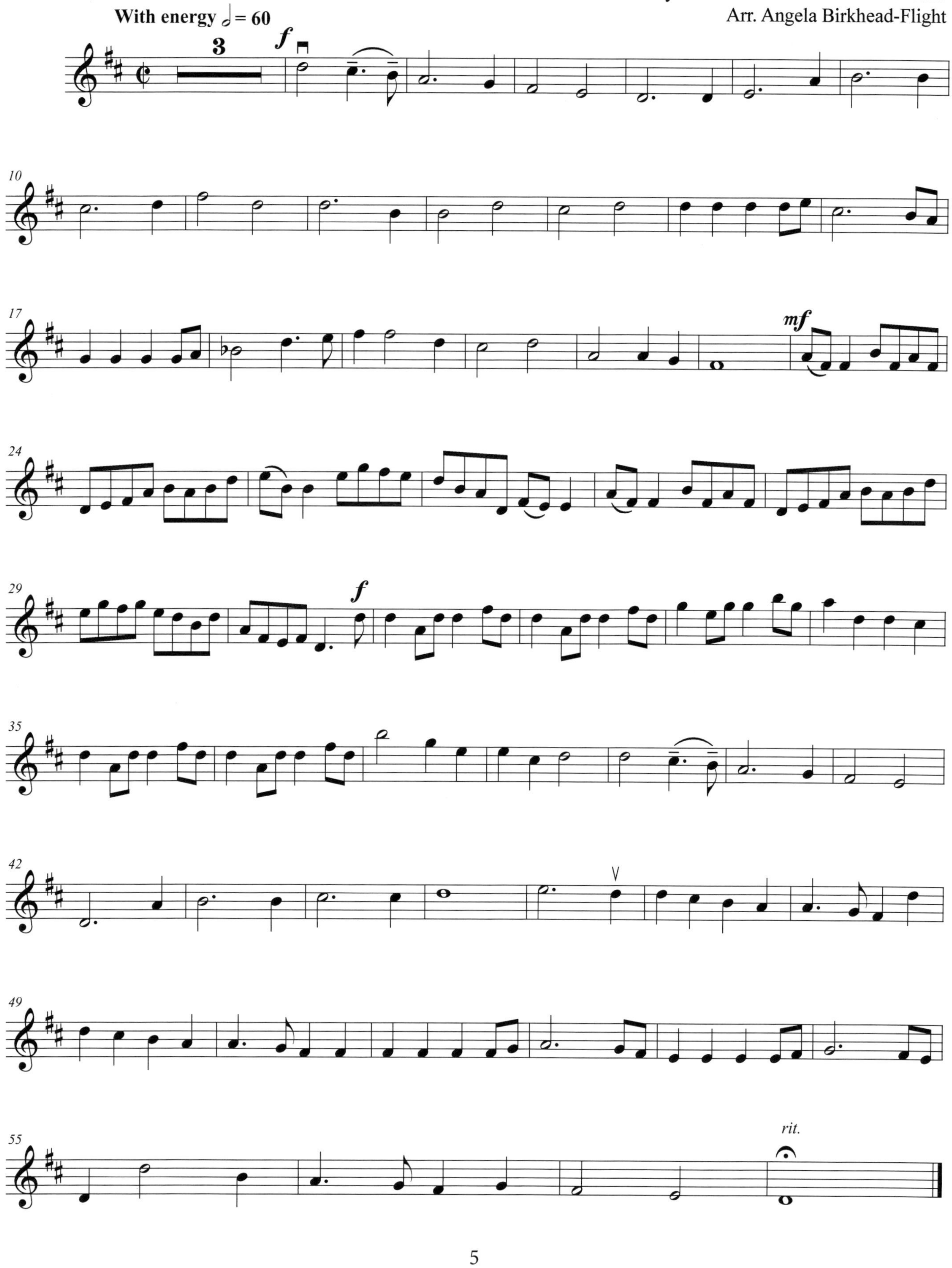

Violin 2

O Come, O Come Emmanuel

French, 15th century
Arr. Angela Birkhead-Flight

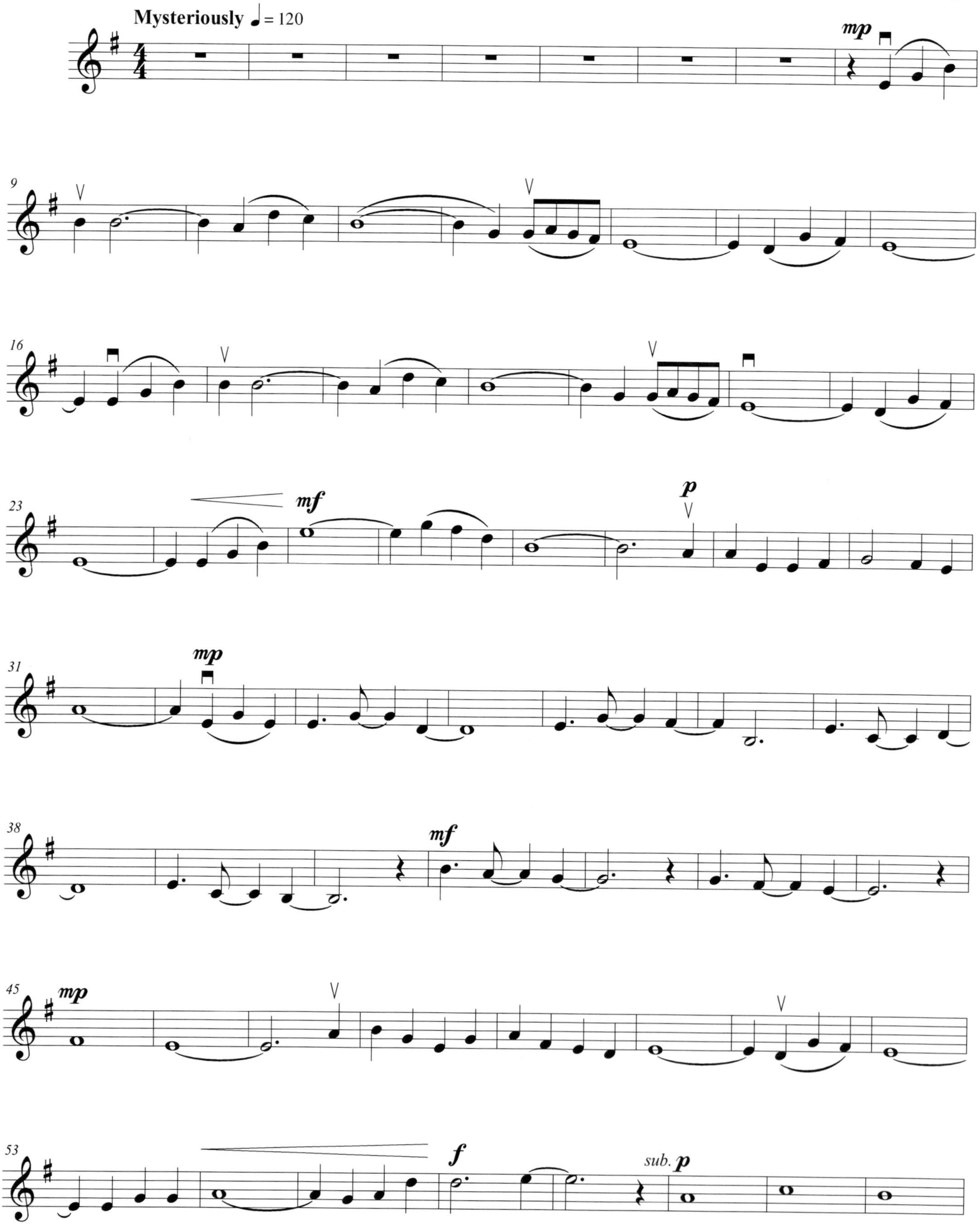

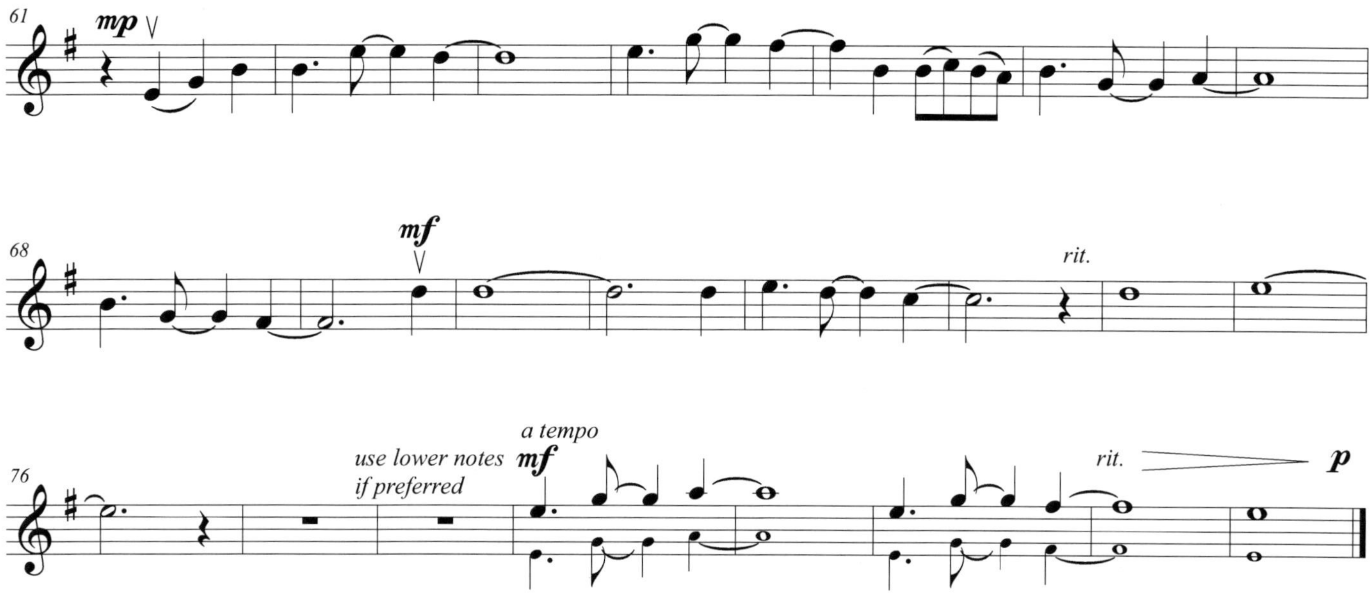
61
mp
68
mf
rit.
76
use lower notes
if preferred
a tempo
mf
rit.
p

Violin 2

Pat-a-Pan

Bernard de La Monnoye (1641–1728)
Arr. Angela Birkhead-Flight

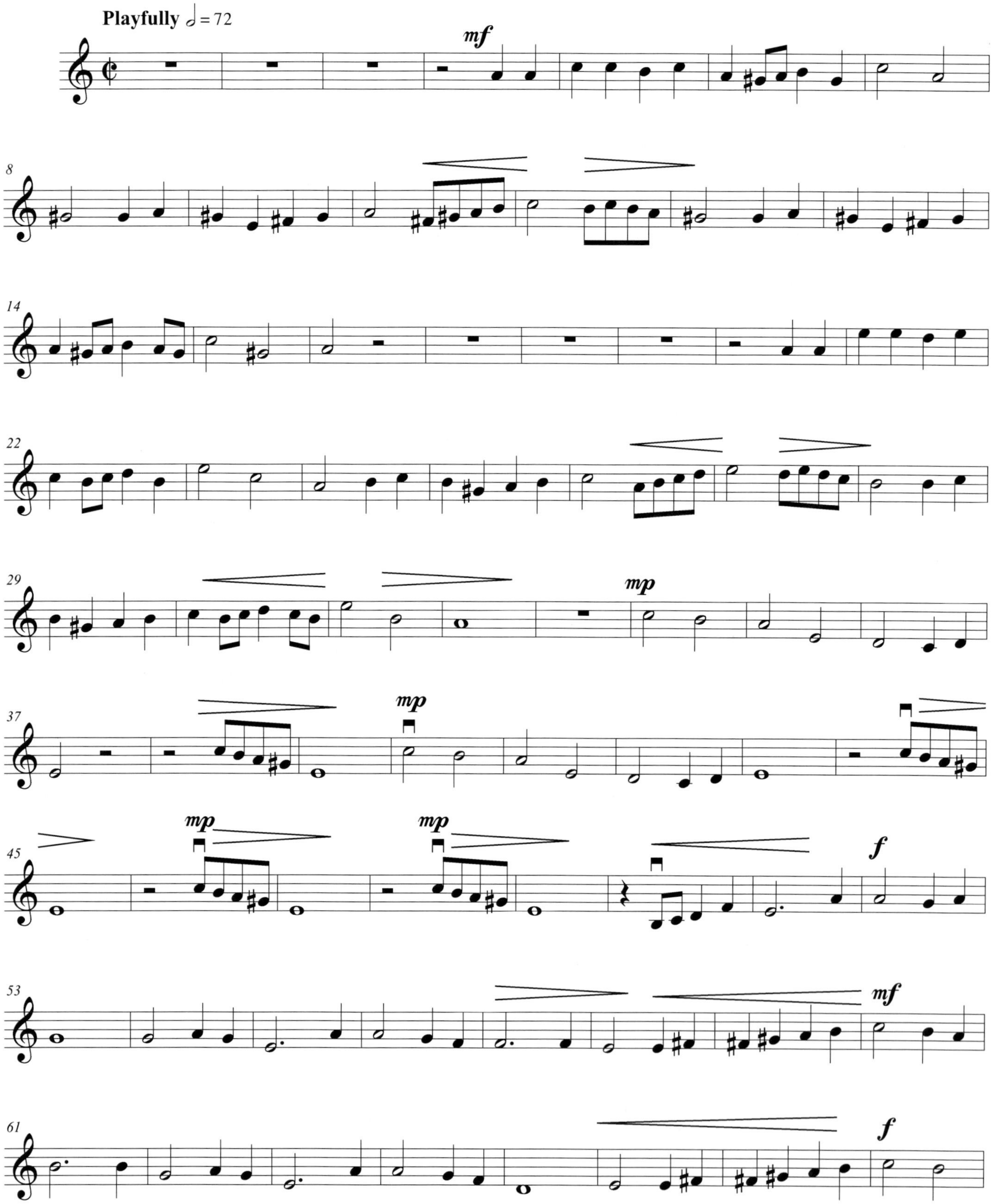

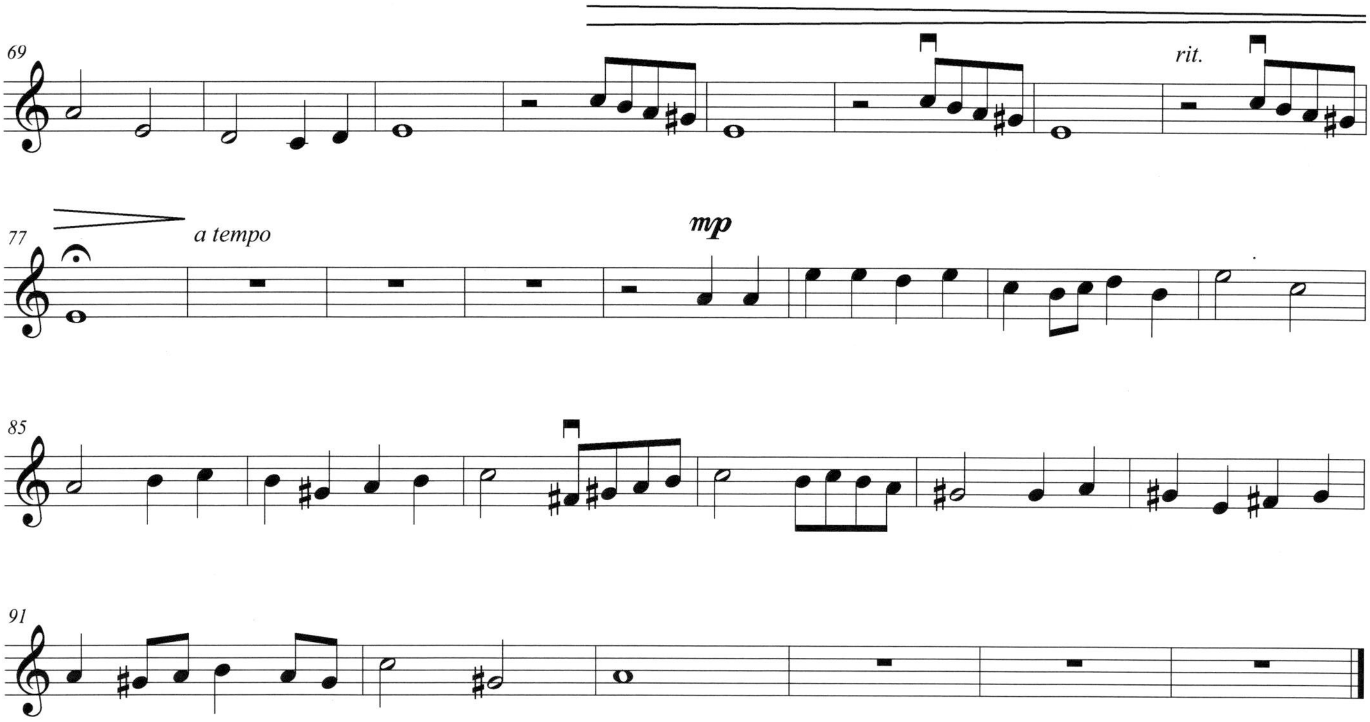
69
rit.
77
a tempo
mp
85
91

Gabriel's Message / Cold Frosty Morning

Basque Folk Carol / American Fiddle Tune
Arr. Angela Birkhead-Flight

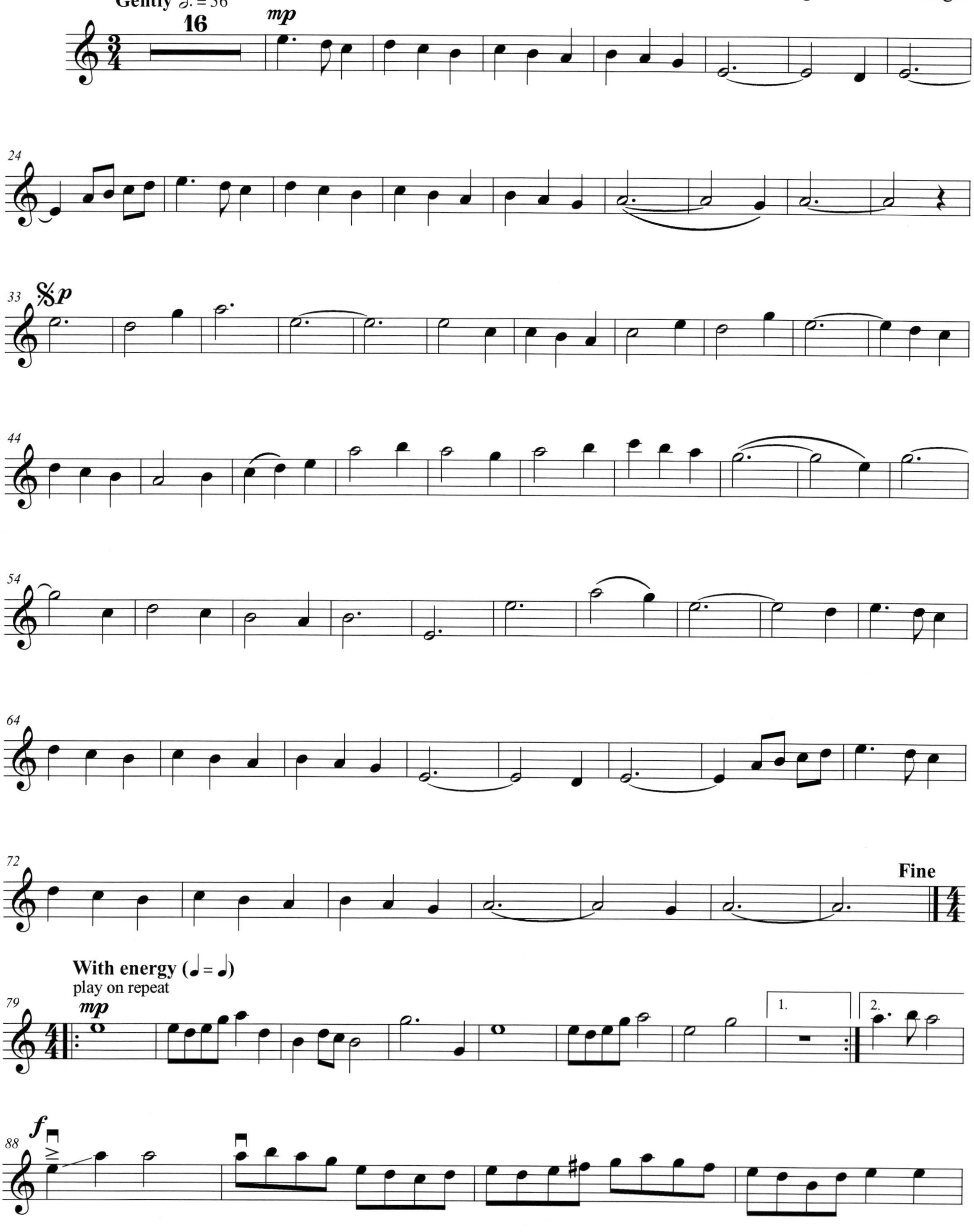

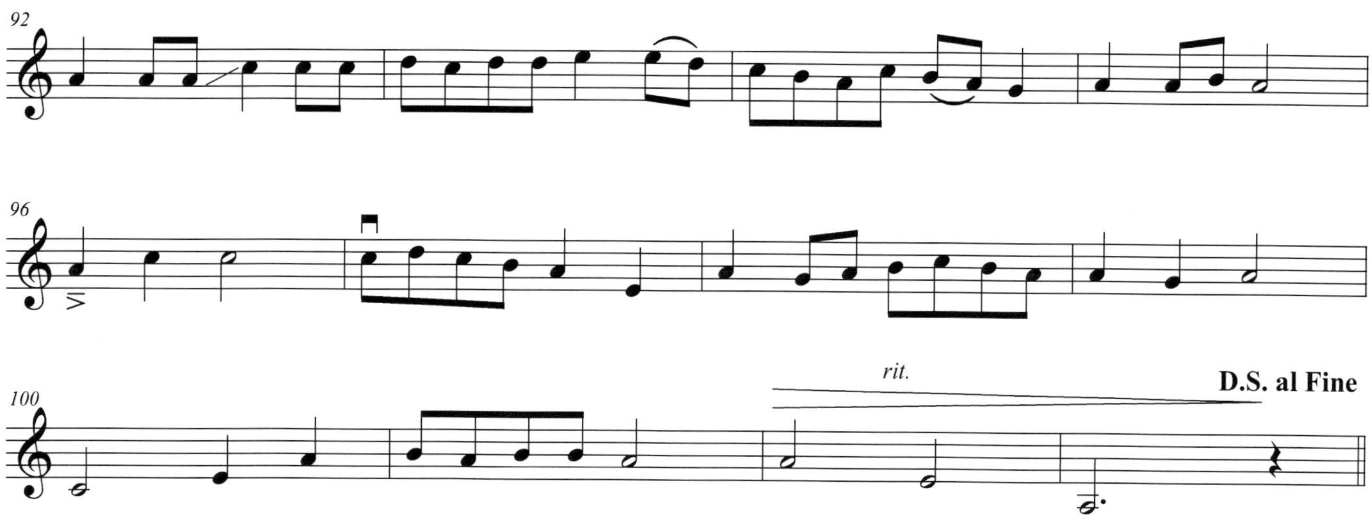
92
96
100
rit.
D.S. al Fine

Violin 2

Angels We Have Heard on High

Traditional French Carol
Arr. Angela Birkhead-Flight

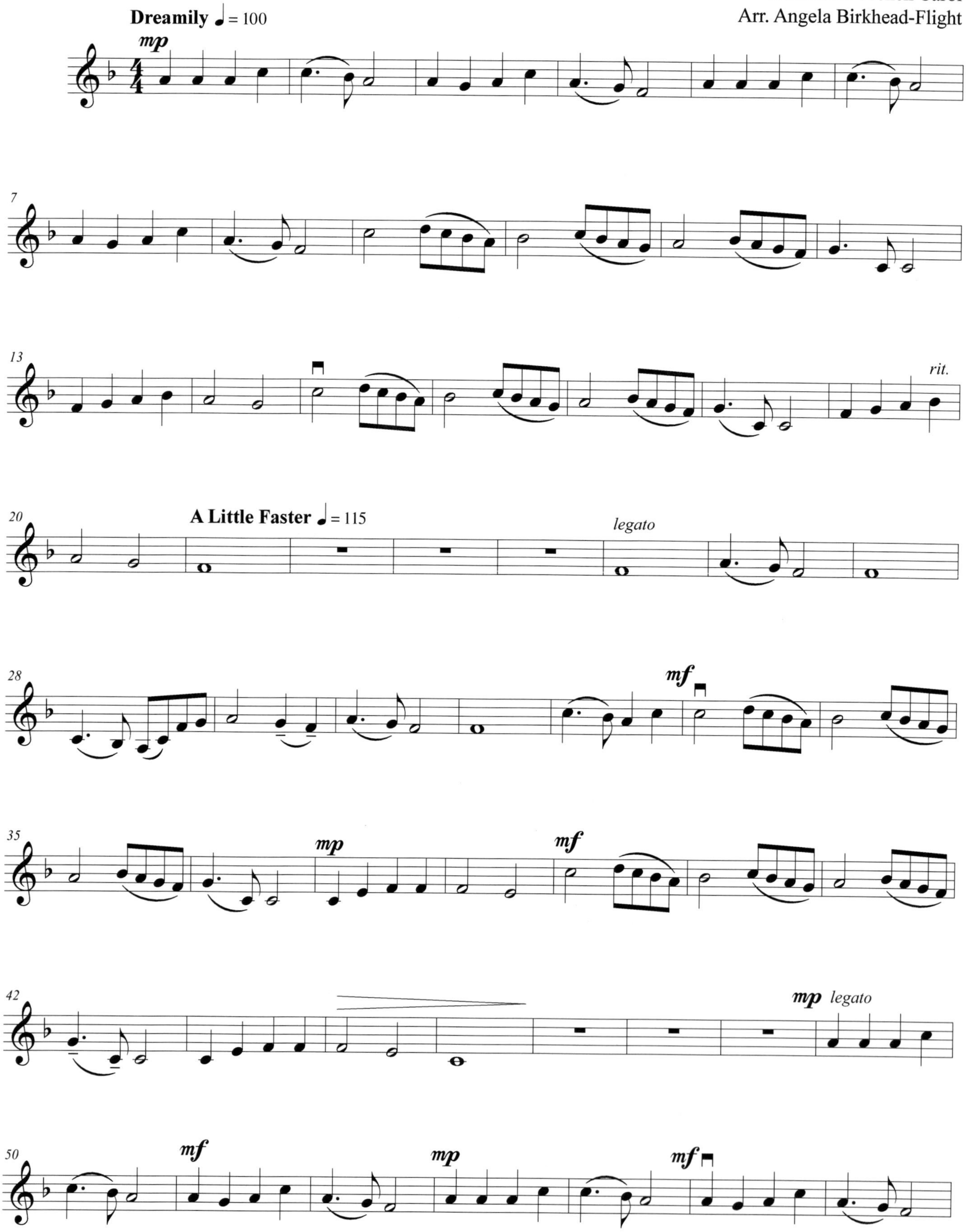

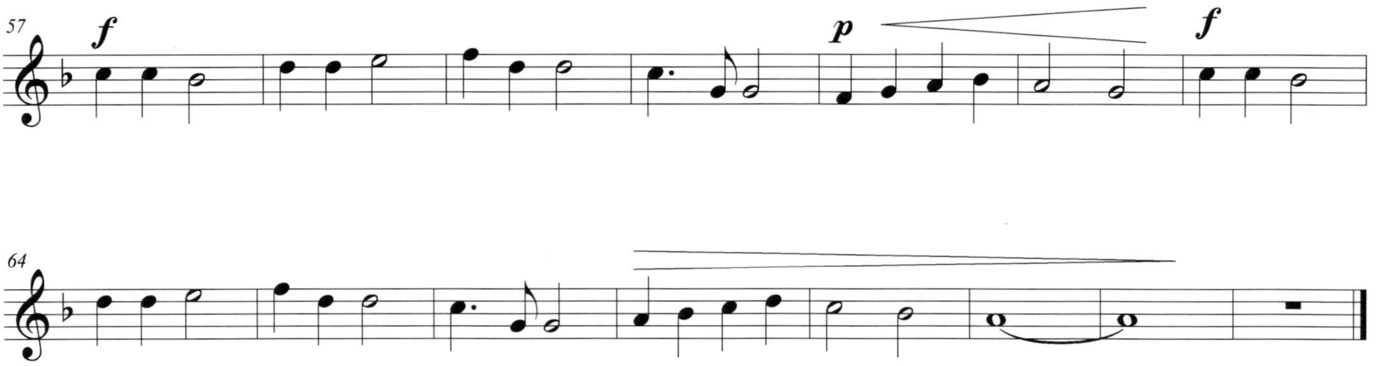
57
f
p
f
64

Violin 2

Silent Night

Franz Gruber
Arr. Angela Birkhead-Flight

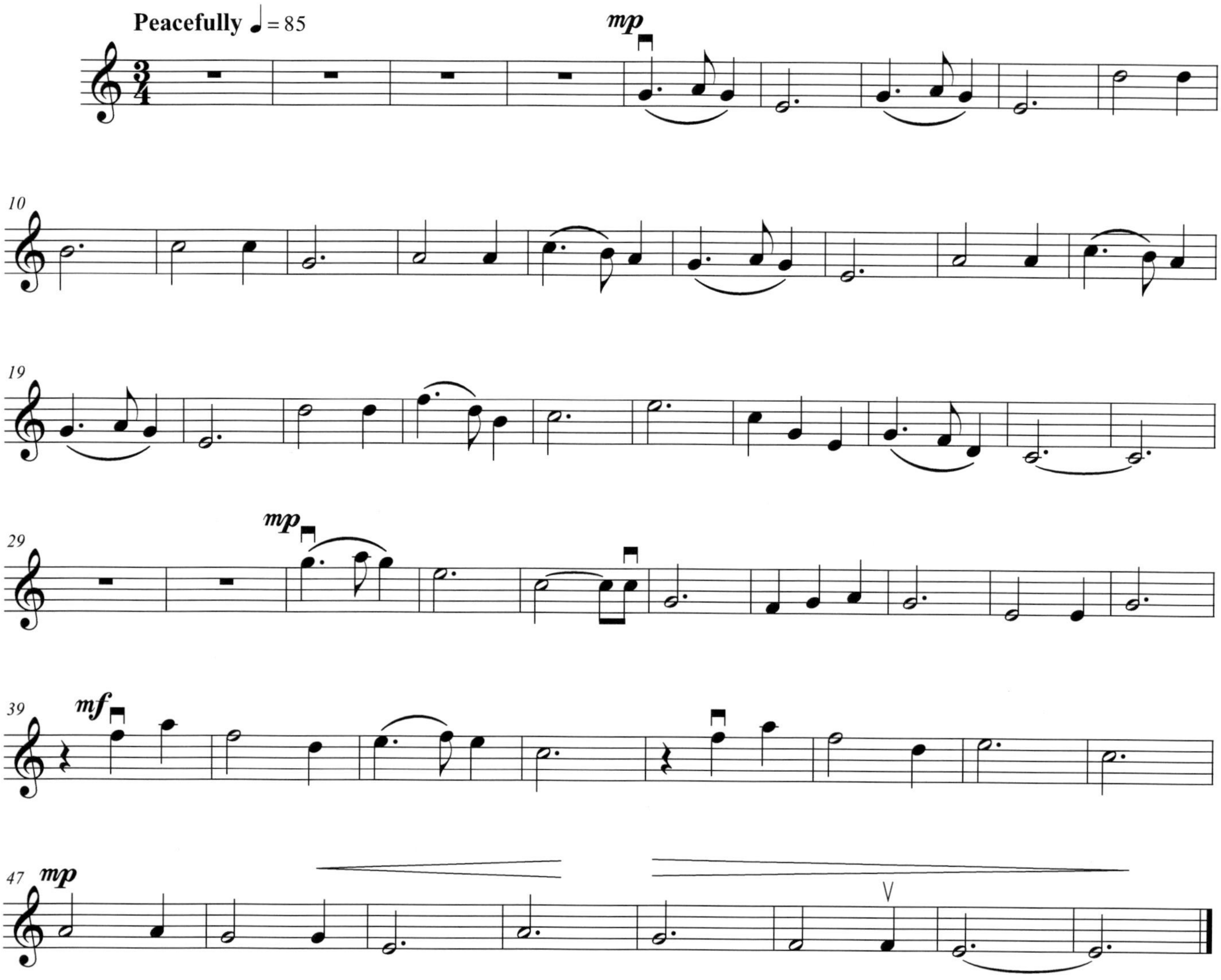

Violin 2

Snowfall

Inspired by Gymnopédie No. 1
by Erik Satie
Angela Birkhead-Flight

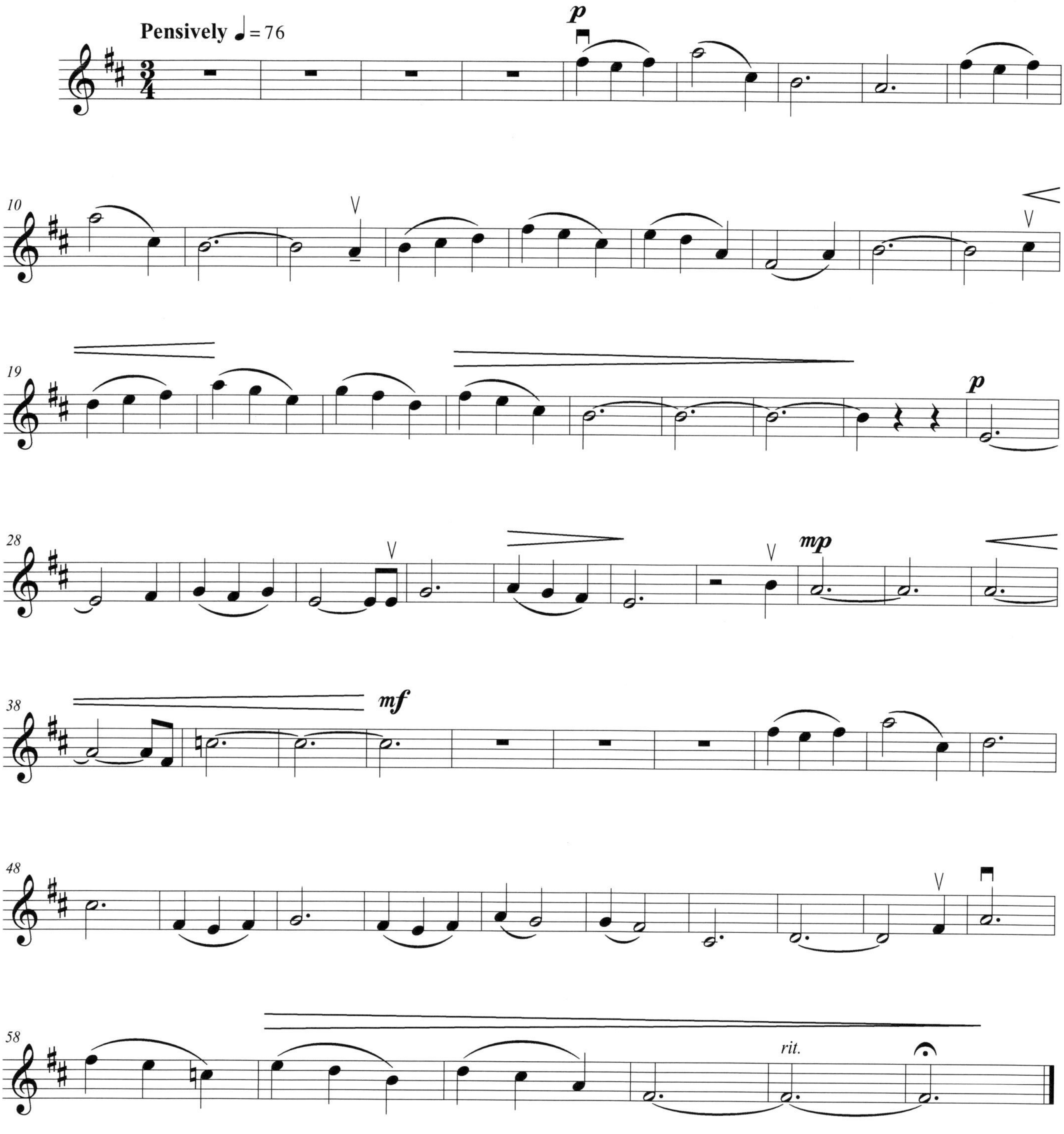

Violin 2

St. Basil's Hymn

Traditional Greek

Arr. Angela Birkhead-Flight

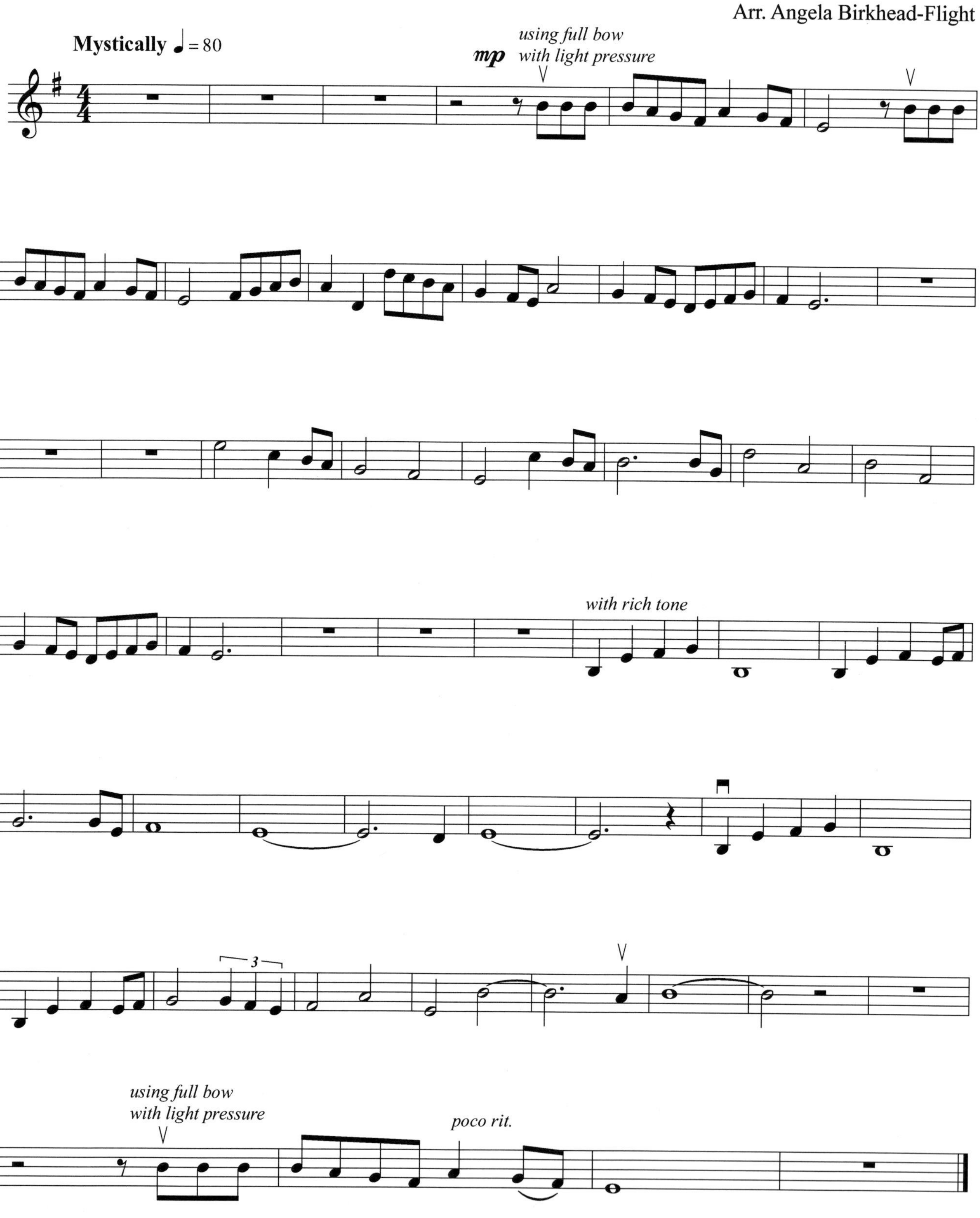

This page has been left blank to avoid an awkward page turn.

Violin 2

O Holy Night

Adolphe Adam
Arr. Angela Birkhead-Flight

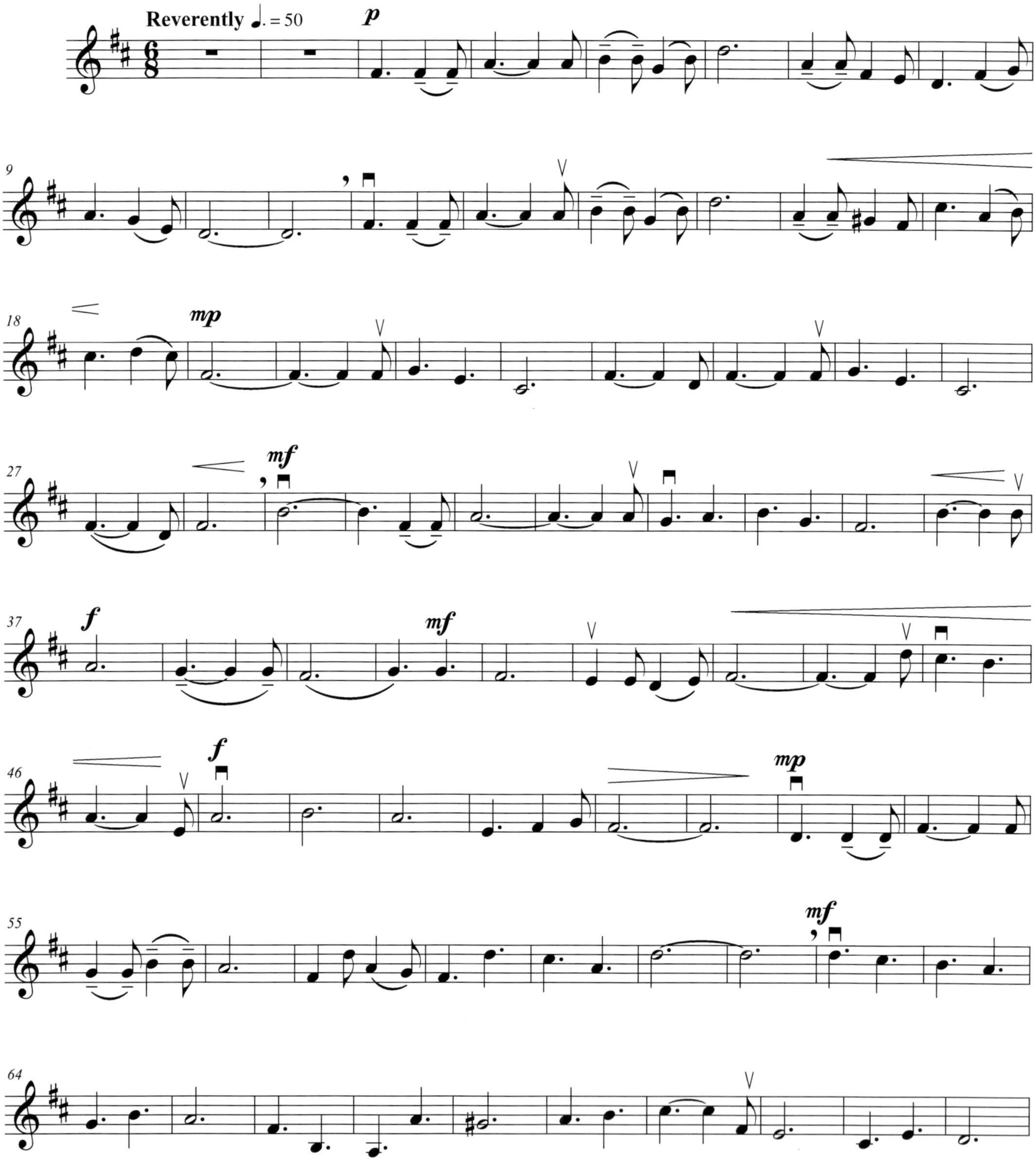

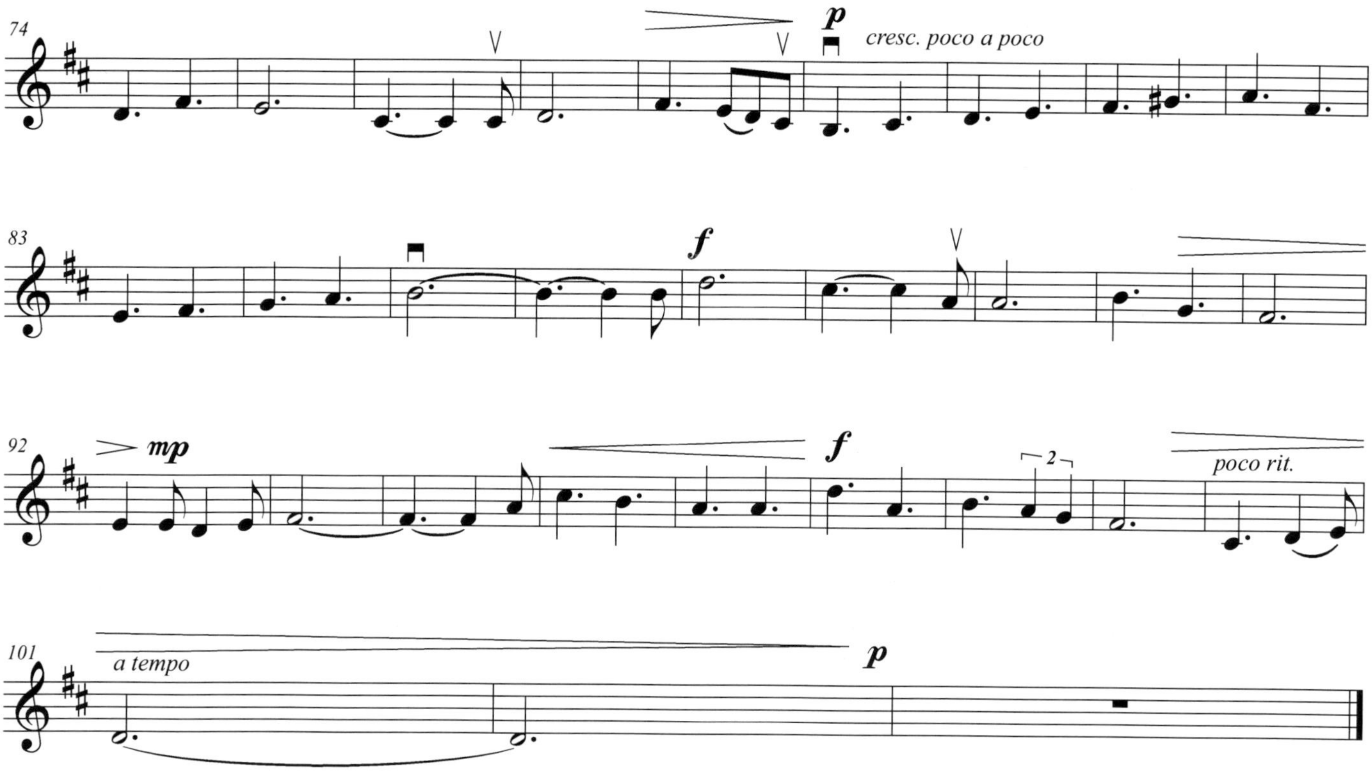
74
p
cresc. poco a poco
83
f
92
mp
f
poco rit.
101
a tempo
p

Violin 2

What Child Is This?

16th century English melody
Arr. Angela Birkhead-Flight

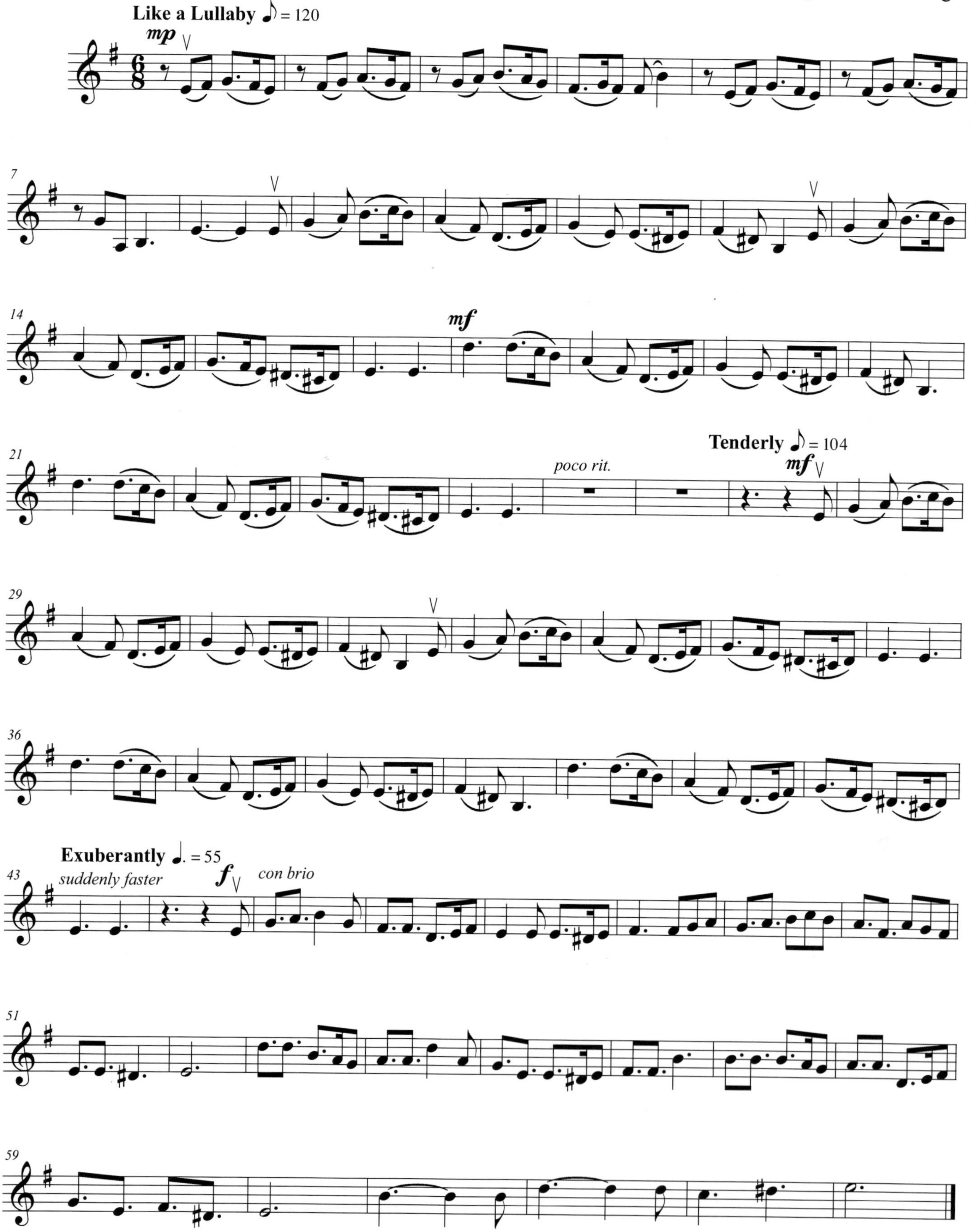